Gene & Dorothy:

A 70 Year Love Story

Roberta Allbert Dayer, Ph. D.,
Editor

Bootstrap Publishing Institute

480-560-4933 Arizona

585-342-0795 New York

mkd@bootstrappublising.net

www.Bootstrappublishing.net

No part of this book may be reproduced in any form or by any electronic or mechanical means, including information storage or retrieval systems, without permission in writing from the publisher.

First edition

ISBN :9781537777030

Library of Congress Catalog Number

Mary K Dougherty at RocCity Book Publishing is Professional, supportive and individualized guidance for writing, marketing or publishing your book! We can now make virtual writer author consultations via SKYPE! To arrange a free 20-minute talk and/or question-and-answer session for your class, please email publisher@bootstrappublishing.net

The Jacket format and design of this book is protected by© RocCity Book Publishing Manufacturing in the United States of America

DEDICATION

This book is dedicated to my dear sisters, Margaret Clarke, and Ruth Rogers, and to our wonderful children and grandchildren, who are the beneficiaries of Gene and Dorothy's teachings and love. I also thank my patient and devoted husband of 60 years, Dr. Roger S. Dayer, who cheerfully endured the absences of a distracted partner while "Gene and Dorothy" came into being. I hope that together, we can create another 70-year love story!

*For Rachael,
With all good wishes,
Roberta
9/29/17*

INTRODUCTION

Gene & Dorothy: A 70 Year Love Story

I hear my mother Dorothy's voice, day and night, even though I now, am eighty-one and she has been gone for sixteen years. Occasionally, when I was a little girl, Mother would cry out in the middle of the night, having a nightmare. Then I would hear my father Gene's voice - - - strong, comforting, reassuring. And Momma (and I) would go back to sleep.

My grown children, who called my parents: "Nana and Boppa", also regularly report on hearing Nana and Boppa's voices, often in humorous ways. Larry, the oldest, remembered that as a child at his grandparents' house, "the garage would always need cleaning and we would always have to make sure we did a good job, or Mrs. A would get after us." In fact, Nana and Boppa became alternate parents to our three children while my husband and I pursued busy, demanding careers. Many of our friends who did not have parents near-by, also called Gene and Dorothy "Nana and Boppa", because they were the kind of people who reached out to those in need; who always were willing to help family, friends and neighbors.

What follows is the seventy-year love story of Gene and Dorothy's journey; from childhood to death; from the barren and poor New Mexico frontier of their youth to the sophisticated and wealthy society of California where they spent their last years. In many ways, their journey mirrors American history in the 20th century, a period in which the United States was transformed from a young nation into the World's super power. Gene and Dorothy lived through two World Wars, the Korean and Vietnam War and the first Iraq war. Their children were born during the Great Depression of the 1930s and became adults in the prosperous years of post-World War II America. While Gene and Dorothy never became directly involved in politics, they followed national events closely and they remained intensely patriotic throughout their lives.

    I serve as Editor - - - the one who has collected, read, organized and interpreted the diaries, records, writings and photos which the Allberts carefully saved and preserved over their long years of marriage. For the most part, Dorothy and Eugene speak for themselves. It is their clear, secure and courageous voices which I hope to communicate. Although I am a trained historian, I did not have to do extensive research for this project because my parents carefully preserved their records from childhood until death: Report cards, school materials, photos, date books, scrapbooks, travel and expense records, writings and autobiographies. In 1948, Dorothy began keeping a daily diary, a practice she continued (with some interruptions) until 1991, when she could no longer write, due to blindness. At that juncture, my father took over the writing; coached by Dorothy. He began compiling the annual Christmas letter, plus writing weekly essays for an Adult Education writing class, plus writing autobiographies of himself and Dorothy. He annexed a family tree to his autobiography and also compiled a lengthy list of all of their travels. Gene and Dorothy visited all forty-eight contiguous states and Hawaii. In addition, since Eugene pursued photography as a hobby, a multitude of photos are available to illustrate their story. Because I was in almost daily contact with my parents until 1987 (when they moved from Buffalo to California), I well remember many of the events and incidents described below. The first two chapters largely are drawn from the Autobiographies and Eugene's essays, which were written in the 1990s, long after the described events took place. However, as the reader soon will recognize, Gene and Dorothy both possessed fantastic memories, which they continually re-enforced by referring to their early records. After 1947, I have largely drawn this story from Dorothy's diaries, Gene's autobiography and my own and my sisters' memories. It is my hope that Gene and Dorothy's lives will inspire their grandchildren, great grandchildren and other readers to take courage from their example; that it will provide guidance and encouragement to all of us who try to live meaningful lives in the 21st century.

TABLE OF CONTENTS

Gene and Dorothy McGrady Allbert, 1908-2000
A 70 Year Love Story

Dedication	3
Introduction	5
Chapter I: Childhood and Adolescence, Raton, New Mexico and Council Bluffs, Iowa	11
Chapter II: Life in Turtle Creek, Pa, 1927-1947	43
Chapter III: Life in Buffalo, New York, 1947-1957: Expanding Horizons	69
Chapter IV: Life Begins at 48! 1958-1973	111
Chapter V: Retirement Years, 1973-1987: A Taste of Luxury	141
Chapter VI: Life in California: Villa Serena, 1987-2000: Final Years	176
Conclusion	210
Epilogue: Living Without Dorothy, 2000-2009	214
List of Photos	221
Acknowledgments	225

CHAPTER I

EUGENE: [Autobiography, 2002 and Essays, 1990s]

The Memoir writing class I started to attend in 1987 caused me to think about writing a record of my life. I thought I should begin with some report on my parents, those people who brought me into the world and nurtured me. Their standards became mine, and guides for my living. Their genes determined my physical characteristics and mental capacity.. The story of my early life comes from memories and conversations I overheard when Mother died and other relations talked.

The Allbert family became New Mexico residents in this way: Alva W. Allbert was in poor health and living along the Kansas-Nebraska border. He went to New Mexico for health reasons and worked as a carpenter in Gardiner, New Mexico [a mining town] in the 1890s, just how long I do not know. He taught school in Maxwell, New Mexico; was Principal of the Springer, New Mexico schools; and then came to Raton and worked in two hardware stores.

His first marriage was to a school sweetheart, Esgena Franklin, from Nebraska. They had a son, Donald, and shortly thereafter, Dad's wife died and Donald went to live with his grandparents in Nebraska.

Alva's second wife was Louise Kelley. She had moved from Peoria, Illinois, when her father, a railroad engineer, had

.0gone to Raton, New Mexico to work on the Santa Fe Railroad. This was about 1903. They met in the First Baptist Church, miles away from their birthplaces, and were married August 28, 1904. The Kelley family went back to Peoria later. Theresa Kelley, Louise's sister, married Frank Stevens and stayed in Raton.

The first child born to Alva and Louise was stillborn. The second child was a boy named Lohr. He was an active, bright child who, while playing on the second floor of their home, fell from a window onto a coal pile. Although apparently not hurt, he died about a year later at the age of four.

Eugene Franklin was born on October 18, 1908, when Lohr was two years old. I do not remember my older brother Lohr, nor do I remember my grandfather Ruben Kelley. I never saw my father's parents. My brother, Churchill Kenneth, was born on January 24, 1912 and Vernon Paul was born November 15, 1914, all of us in Raton, New Mexico.

EDITOR

The great era of railway building, which began after the Civil War, resulted in the completion of the first transcontinental railway in 1869 and continued well into

the 20th century. Raton, with its pass through the mountains, developed as a major link in railways going East and West. Located in the northeast corner of New Mexico, Raton was surrounded by coalmines. While many of the local people were Indians or Mexicans, neither are mentioned in the Allbert records nor in other memoirs, such as "The Gardiner, New Mexico Story" by F. Stanley. Nor did Gene and Dorothy ever talk about these residents of New Mexico. Italian immigrants were imported to work in the coalmines and negroes were brought in from Alabama during a railroad strike. [David F. Myrick, *New Mexico's Railroads*, 1990] New Mexico did not become a state until 1912, four years after Eugene was born.

This was an era when white racial supremacy was unquestioned, despite the Civil War, which officially had ended slavery in the United States. However, racial segregation was accepted in varying degrees in the United States until after the Second World War and the great civil rights struggle of the 1960s. Very few people talked or wrote about the rights of negroes, Mexicans or American Indians.

When Eugene was born, Theodore Roosevelt still was President, soon to be succeeded by William Howard Taft in 1909. While the Allbert family, like most middle westerners, were firm Republicans, religion played a much more important role in their lives than did politics. Nationalism and patriotism formed part of the fabric of their lives.

EUGENE: [Autobiography, 2002 and Essays, 1990s]

My earliest recollection of Dad's work is when he was a bookkeeper for the Raton Water Company. I am told that I was born in a house called the Lob House in the northern part of Raton at the mouth of Railroad Canyon. The Santa Fe Trail was in this area. The first place I remember living was on North Third Street, and one of the first events was Dad taking me over to see a wildcat Mr. Andrews had in a cage in his backyard.

The Alva Allberts' next move was to 800 South Second Street in Raton.... Our house at 800 South Second Street was in the last block of houses on the street. We lived one block from the area where circuses were held. The elephants and other animals all passed the front of our house when they went for water. The fenced-in backyard had a woodshed at the back on the Cimmaron Avenue side. Next to it was a small shed where Dad and Mother kept a cow for a short time. Along the side fence was a row of Carolina poplar trees and behind the lot was an alley, then a hill probably 30 feet high. This was a fine place to fly kites. Our house did not have electricity; we used kerosene lamps for light at night.

There were a number of children near our house: Next door was Mary Ellen Schmidt. Two things I remember about her: she once hit me with her toy hoe and put a nick in my forehead. I must have thrown rocks over the fence at her, because her brother told me he would cut off my ears if I didn't stop. Three girls lived across Cimmaron Avenue. Ruth and Marie lived in the brick house on Second Street; Ruby lived in the house behind them. My sex education started when I played house with them. I don't remember this occurring but once, but I got the idea.

Living in a small, four room house with cold, running water in the kitchen, kerosene oil lamps and a pit toilet in the back yard could not have been an easy life for my parents, Louise and Alva, but it was not unusual in Raton, Territory of New Mexico, when I arrived in 1908. I used to hear mother describe getting rid of bed bugs behind the quarter-rounds and the wallpaper when they moved in. After Lohr's death, I was an only child until my brother, Kenneth, was born when I was three. I suspect that mother and papa doted on their chubby little blue-eyed boy with the unruly blond hair, but they were not demonstrative and displays of affection were rare. But for an energetic, adventurous little boy, the mountains of New Mexico were a wondrous place to grow up!

I liked to watch mother as she did her many chores. The weekly routine rarely varied - - - washing on Monday, ironing on Tuesday. Washing clothes followed a primitive procedure, which took most of the day. A stand with a place on each side for washtubs and a hand crank wringer between them was set up in the center of the kitchen. A copper boiler was put on the kitchen range and half filled with water. The reservoir on the right side of the range heated water that was put into the tubs. A bar of laundry soap was cut into thin strips and put in one tub. The white clothes were put into the washtub and any spots removed on the wash board. A cone shaped plunger, on the end of a wood handle, was used to move the water through the clothes.

The clothes were then put through the wringer and put into the boiler. After boiling, the white clothes went into the rinse water. After stirring by hand or the plunger, these were again put through the wringer and taken outside and hung on the steel clothes lines and held in place with clothes pins. The dark clothes were washed in the soapy water and stubborn spots were removed on the wash board. These were rinsed, wrung again and hung out to dry. Some of the white things were blued and collars and cuffs starched. Water was bailed from the tubs and poured around the vegetation in the yard. All the things were put away and the floor mopped in time to start dinner, the noon meal. In the winter the clothes froze dry.

After wash day came Tuesday. It was ironing day. Several handle less irons were put on the hottest part of the stove to heat. The ironing board was set up and the dampened clothes to be ironed were put on the table part of the kitchen cabinet. A handle that had a clip on the bottom was taken from the drawer in the cabinet. Mother wet her finger with her tongue and tested the iron [to see if it was hot enough] she had lifted from the stove with the handle for temperature. If satisfied, she spread the first piece to be ironed over the board and, after checking the bottom of the iron for cleanliness, started her work. Even after we had electricity in Gardiner, this process continued until electric irons were available.

The Santa Fe Railroad tracks were a short distance beyond First Street. The trains were just picking up speed when they passed the 800 block (where we lived). Dad's sister, Ida, had married the Governor of Kansas. They visited us and I was given a silver dollar.

When I was five years old our family and a couple who lived in the middle of our block rented a team of horses and a wagon and went up Sugarite canyon to Walton's ranch to camp for a week. The distance was about 15 miles and probably took all day.

The log cabin where we stayed had probably been used for farm help to sleep in during haying season. All I remember of staying at the cabin was that some small animals ran across our faces at times when we were asleep. There was a trout stream running through the valley. The neighbor for some reason spanked me. I probably deserved it, but Dad bawled him out about it.

We often visited relatives who lived nearby and went on picnics together. One Fourth of July, Uncle Frank Stevens drove the Raton Supply Company wagon up to Blossburg Canyon where after our noon meal we noticed the clouds---a storm was coming. We loaded up and went home as fast as possible, about three miles. The storm hit with a vengeance and a lot of hail fell. After the storm, Dad took a galvanized wash tub out to the front yard and almost filled it with hailstones. Mother prepared the ingredients for ice cream. The ice cream freezer used the hail to freeze the mix and in a little while there was ice cream for all.

In 1914 Dad took a job as warehouseman in Gardiner, a coalmining town three miles from Raton. Dad had to stay at a boarding house in Gardiner during the week and came home on the weekends. The St. Louis, Rocky Mountain and Pacific Company for whom he worked was building two new houses in Gardiner, one for the mine clerk, Mr. Dennis, and one for Dad. These

were not ready in the fall of 1914, so Mother and her three sons took a trip east to Peoria, Illinois to her Mother's home. Grandmother Kelley's two-story house had a unique heating system for the second floor. The room where we slept had a grilled opening in the floor in the corner of the room. The heat from the first floor came into the room through this opening. Another use for this opening was for communication. At breakfast time the call went out: "breakfast will soon be ready"! We would make our final preparations and hurry downstairs.

While in Peoria I went to school for the first grade and was the tallest boy in my class. Two of Mother's sisters and one brother still lived at home. As I remember it, two cousins, boys about my age, also lived there. One of my cousins, Robert Kelley, showed me how to hitch a ride with his sled to the back of a buggy. We ran to one and pulled one end of a rope over the back axle of the buggy. The other end of the rope was tied to the sled. We rode for a while until the driver saw us. He snapped the reins against the horse and soon we had to let go because we travelled too fast.

While we were gone, Dad had started a Sunday School in the school house in Gardiner. It met on Sunday afternoons. In the spring of 1915, we moved into our new house in Gardiner. This was the beginning of a new kind of life. Our new house had a bathtub and electricity. The house faced north toward the two-room school house, and behind it was a mountain with a cliff halfway up and topped with a big rock shaped like a sheep. The west side of the house faced the canyon and on the south side was a rail siding, then a dry bed of a creek, then a gentle slope to the mountains on the other side of the valley.

The Dennis family lived on the east side of us. They had two children, Clara and William, both older than I. They also had a horse. Across the street and to the west a Scotch family lived. They had a daughter, Martha, and a horse and buggy. The summer between first and second grade seemed so long; there didn't seem much to do. I was supposed to take a nap. Sometimes I would sneak out the window and visit a man who worked in a small building behind the Dennis house. He ground coke to dust, passed it through a fine screen and then put it into shallow dishes in what looked like a large fireplace. I suppose he was checking it for carbon and rock content. Bill Dennis let me ride his horse. I wasn't a good rider, and fell off at times. Bill also had a 22 rifle. I pestered Dad to get me a gun and after two years I got one for Christmas. We shot at tin cans, bottles, birds and snakes. About 5:00 p.m. one evening I shot at a bird on the electric light pole. I missed the bird but cut the line to our house. Dad had to get the electrician to reconnect the line! I don't remember his remarks to me.

Second grade was held in the room with the first grade. The teacher was Miss Sylvia Potial. She was a new teacher. She had blond hair a fair complexion and was slightly plump. I later learned that Miss Potial had just graduated from the State Normal School. It was not

long before I was disciplined for talking to Lucy Palazzi. Miss Potial told me to sit next to Lucy in one of the double desks if I wanted to talk to her. I was embarrassed but did as I was told and I didn't have to sit with Lucy again.

At that time, we had thirty-minute recesses. This gave us time to play Run Sheep Run and other such games. There were other opportunities at this school, such as climbing the mountain behind the building. It was only about 200 feet away and there was a quarry about 500 feet up the mountain, easily reached in ten minutes by energetic boys.

There were times when it seemed appropriate to have a rock fight. These didn't last long and as I remember, those who were hit with stones were not

badly hurt. I don't remember any reprimands from the teachers about this action.

Harold Lowe was in the fourth grade when I first met him. Harold seemed able to make friends well. About a year later we played together at school and he invited me to come over to his house. Then I learned that he had an older sister and a younger brother. They lived in one of the three room adobe houses, just down the hill from the school. He told me that his father was a mule driver in the coal mine. Harold was a good student and became my best friend. Even though the family seemed poor, he was able to get a clarinet and learn to play it. As he grew a little taller I noticed that he had short legs and a long body. And another thing I found out was that his mother was part Cherokee Indian.

The top of the mountain behind the school house was faced with a cliff on the south side. We enjoyed walking along the cracks from top to bottom that were about 18 inches wide. We liked to go down these cracks by spreading our legs and arms to keep from falling too fast. It was dangerous but somehow, we survived!

There were pinion trees and prickly pear cactus on the lower south side of the mountain. When we could beat the squirrels to the pinion nuts we had some to eat. Also, when the prickly pear fruit was purple, we would take them off, wipe the spines off on our overalls and eat these. We played with sling shots, beanies, boomerangs, one mid-iron golf club, bats and balls. Sometimes we could get steel punching from the machine shop. We could throw these about 200 feet with our slingshots. We

were not very accurate with our throws but there was a lot of open space around our targets.

The warehouse that Dad operated was in half of the Blossburg Mercantile Company Building. The other half was the company general store. The Blossburg Mercantile Company was owned by the coal company. It was a general store and butcher shop. They issued script to the miners when their money ran out and it was paid back from the wages the miners received. Their coal company was non-union. The miners in Colorado had been organized and strikes there were very violent. However, one strike led to the importation of Negro workers who lived under segregated conditions. The saloon created a curtain down the middle so that the mostly Italian workers did not have to drink with the Negroes! [F. Stanley and James E. and Barbara H. Sherman, *Stories of Gardiner, New Mexico*, 1965] The Mercantile Company operated the saloon which was located about one half block behind the store and not too far east of our house.

The First World War had started and coal and coke were in great demand. The company had beehive coke ovens and supplied coke to the Colorado Fuel and Iron Company in Pueblo, Colorado and coal to the Santa Fe Railroad. A new warehouse was built along the railroad spur in front of the Mercantile Co. building. It was the main warehouse for the six mines. Dad was given an assistant. The half of the Mercantile building now vacant was remodeled and made into a motion picture house. The 18th Amendment [Prohibition} closed the saloon and the company made the building into a clubhouse which had a soda fountain, a pool hall and a dance floor. When it was opened we, all had free ice cream cones and a big party.

EDITOR

The first World War began in 1914 in Europe, with Great Britain, France and Russia allied against Germany, Austria /Hungary. President Woodrow Wilson, the Democratic President who had been elected in 1912 when Theodore Roosevelt split the Republican Party and ran on an independent ticket, was determined to keep the United States out of the war. However, as the war dragged on and German submarines began attacking American vessels, the President finally declared war on Germany in April,1917, promising to "make the world safe for democracy". Aside from increasing demand for coal, the war seemed to have made little impression on the Allberts, but some young men in Raton volunteered to serve. The war ended in November, 1918.

After the war, President Wilson led a delegation to the Paris Peace Conference of 1919, where he negotiated the Versailles Peace Treaty, which included plans for a League of Nations aimed at ending war.

When Congressional Republicans denounced the League of Nations, President Wilson traveled by train around the country, seeking popular support for the Versailles Treaty. During this exhausting trip, he suffered a stroke and never returned to normalcy. The Senate defeated the League of Nations and the United States entered a period of isolationism, vowing never again to become involved in European affairs.

EUGENE: (Autobiography)

Dr. Johnson left Gardiner and a new doctor, Dr. James, was employed. A new house for him was built across the street. It had a telephone, flush toilet and six rooms. After about two years we moved into this house.

When I was in 5th grade, my teacher was Miss Manning. She was blond and not too tall. When we were seated at our desks, she talked to us as she put her books in place on top of her desk and put things in the drawers. About the last thing she put in the bottom right-hand drawer was a rawhide whip about 2 ½ feet long. She did not have to use it during the time I was in the fifth, sixth or seventh grades. I visited her many years later and asked whether she had ever used it in school. She said only once.

When I was about ten years old I received, an Erector set for Christmas. This set had a small electric motor in it. Dad gave me a battery to supply power to the motor. I was intrigued with the rotating pulley. I could drive some of the other wheels in the set with it. By the time I had finished high school, I knew there was much more in the electrical field to be learned and applied.

Papa said: "Eugene the coal bin is close to the house and there are only two steps up to the porch. I think you are old enough (I think I was 12) and strong enough to start bringing in the kindling and coal for your Mother." He continued: "the kindling must be small enough to catch fire easily and short enough to go into the stove. Put it in the box behind the range. There should be a bucket of coal near the stove morning and evening, so your Mother will be able to do her cooking." Growing older had its obligations and the assignment was interesting at first. The axe was heavy, but the wood easy to cut. The coal bucket taxed my strength when I tried to lift it. Again, I found it possible. The problem was it had to be done morning and night. Soon spring came and Papa had some other instructions. "It is almost time to plant the garden. Your Mother will need the ground spaded so she can plant the seeds. Eugene, there is a spading fork on the back porch you can use to turn over the soil in the garden area." Responsibility came easy to me and this early training made accepting assignments a challenge.

We all attended the Baptist church and Sunday School in Raton and the evangelistic meetings that were held there in a tent each summer. The Chautauqua had a week's program occasionally, and we attended some of these. One subject, "It Pays to Advertise", is about all I remember of these. When I was twelve years old I accepted Christ as my savior and was baptized and joined the Southern Baptist Church. It became the center of our social life. In my early teens, Dad was the director of the Intermediate Baptist Young People's Union (BYPU) and mother was director of the Junior BYPU. The BYPU had some sort of social about every six weeks. Most of them were held in the Church basement and were well supervised. I had learned to drive the car by this time but was not entrusted with it.

I think I was 13 when I joined the Boy Scouts. Dad bought me the Scout uniform and hat and I went to the Scout camp at Ute Park for 10 days. Dad had tried to get me to play the piano. A teacher came from Raton to show me how. I had no inclination to practice, even though Mother insisted it was necessary. Later, when a band was formed among the miners. Dad purchased a baritone horn and I worked at it for a while in order to try out for the band but I lost interest. Outdoor play was much more fun!

There were only a few students for the eighth grade class in Gardiner so they were sent to the Raton School along with those who were in high school. A truck with canvas sides and benches was used as a bus. We carried our lunches and school books. Manual training was part of the eighth grade curriculum and I enjoyed it. Our teacher was able to show the proper use of tools, how to sharpen them and gave us projects to make. The best of mine was a keyed mortise and Tenon joint. In high school, I made a bookend out of mahogany. The grain was open and when I stained it the open grain showed white. My instructor told me to sand off the stain, use wood filler and stain again. These lessons need to be learned only once. My next project was an oak pedestal. It took most of the year to finish it.

I did not enjoy studying Latin but physics was

interesting. The Latin teacher was also interested in manners. One morning she lectured each of her classes on how to tip your hat or cap, say hello and many other items.

Senior year we studied chemistry and trigonometry which were hard for me but I continued to enjoy industrial arts. Three of us were assigned to make a drawing of the High School building and show modifications to obtain better use of the building. I was to make the floor plan; Arthur Kelly to show the elevations and Willard Krueger would make the perspectives. We took our study hall times and any other time we could squeeze out and did it.

Dad Allbert had not had a vacation since he went to Illinois in 1917. Besides his work, he was very interested in his church and education. The Southern Baptist Churches of New Mexico had been given an opportunity to buy a resort hotel just north of Las Vegas, New Mexico, for use as a college. They had scheduled a meeting at this hotel to discuss the issue before going any further with the proposal. Dad thought this was an opportunity for the family to attend the meeting and have a pleasant camping trip after it.

The family owned a Model T Ford touring car. Dad made a chest to fasten to the running board. This would hold our food and cooking utensils. He thought we should have one of those fancy new tents, which had a flap that would fasten over the car. It would have a canvas floor and provide a place to live while we were on the trip. Mother purchased a two-burner gasoline stove for cooking. It was only 110 miles to Las Vegas and a few miles farther to the Montezuma Hotel. It took us all day to

drive there and find a place to camp on the grounds. Dad and Mother, with my help, soon had our tent set up and we had supper.

We three boys wanted to be on our way to camp at the base of Red River Pass. Most of the roads had been located above 6000 feet elevation. The Red River Pass to Marina Valley would be over 10,000 feet elevation, the same as the pass to the Cimarron River Valley. We camped a little way down this valley for two days before going home. I remember the mountains, the switchbacks and eating outdoors. I enjoyed the freedom I felt. Camp chores were easy to do. It was nice to have Mother and Dad with us all the time. I don't even remember having trouble with my brothers. It was a successful vacation.

Mother had a surprise birthday party for me on my fifteenth. When the young people arrived, I was under the car fixing something. I think all the Senior BYPU attended. Mother and Dad had girls from the Raton Baptist Church visit occasionally so we could learn some of the finer things in life. I think we had shown some of our activities to them. We had a 22 rifle and a 12-gauge shotgun for the girls to shoot. Mother prepared good food and Dad served their plates and they were full.

My social life was improving. I started seeing Dorothy McGrady. She was good looking and smart and went to our church activities. Dorothy and I were in the same eighth grade class at school. [Gene had started school at age 7 and Dorothy had been pushed ahead a year.] Since I lived in Gardiner and required time to study, and Dorothy was in Raton, we saw each other only on Sundays and at socials. By the Junior Year, we were going together. At the end of the Junior year, I heard that Dorothy would be leaving Raton and going to live with her father in Council Bluffs, Iowa. I went over to see her and we talked and said goodbye.

The summer of 1926 I worked for Tomlinson Electric and Hardware Company. It was a 7 to 6 job, six days a week except on Saturday when we closed at 9 p.m. It was interesting most of the time. They had open stock on some dishes, and when I had to wash those I was not happy. One of the first service jobs I was sent out on was to repair a vacuum cleaner. I took it all apart and reassembled it, finding no fault. Then I checked the plug where a wire was disconnected. From then on I checked plugs first. I decorated the store windows using our stock and crepe paper.

This year Raton had a new electric generating plant and electricity would be inexpensive, so electric ranges were stocked. Soon electric refrigerators and a new line of washing machines, then radios, all were stocked. Mr. Tomlinson sold electric ranges to replace coal ranges and then sold the coal ranges. We had a lot of

heavy work. We delivered to Sugarite and Dawson [nearby towns] ---two young men to handle the load and all of it for $50 per month. When new stock came in, I would generally price it and many times I would count the money from the cash register on a Saturday night.

Mr. Tomlinson asked me if I could work at the store at noon hour for him during the senior school year and if I could, I would be able to work Saturdays. I agreed to do that and continued to have some money to spend.

In the fall of 1926, Mr. Evans, the master mechanic for the coal company, went to East Pittsburgh, PA to the Westinghouse Electric plant. He stayed with friends in Turtle Creek and visited the plant each day for at least a week. He inquired about apprentice and student courses and learned there was a course for high school graduates. When he returned, he told Dad about it and recommended that I try to get in this course.

Dad wrote to the sales office in Denver and requested application forms. We sent these in to Westinghouse and I was accepted and was to report to work on August 8, 1927. I finished high school in May and worked for Tomlinson until the end of June, preparing to leave about the middle of July. I had written Dorothy and told her I would stop and see her on my way.

It was a sad time for Mother when I left. For Dad, too, I guess but he did not show it much. I went to Kansas City and visited my Aunt Ida Bailey, then took a train to Council Bluffs, Iowa and spent a couple of days with Dorothy. The train at Council Bluffs went right into Peoria, Illinois, and I stayed with many relatives there about ten days. We really partied! I think I gained ten pounds. The next train took me to Pittsburgh where I changed to a local train to East Pittsburgh and to the Westinghouse Electric and Manufacturing Company, as it was known then, August 8, 1927.

DOROTHY: [Autobiography, Dictated to Eugene in 1997]

I was born in Sioux City, Iowa to David Charles McGrady and Sarah Jannette Glassey McGrady on August 14, 1910. My mother was married when she was 18 to David Charles McGrady who was 31---a big age difference. My grandmother, Mary Kendall Glassey, kept a Boarding House for young workingmen which is where

my parents met. My father was a boilermaker for steam engines. "He boarded at Grandmother's" where he met my mother and won her heart. But sadly, not for long. By the time I was three, my mother had left me and father and my grandmother became my primary caregivers. Naturally I could not understand why my mother was gone but my grandmother did the best she could. She taught me good conduct, good morals and a desire to improve my station in life. My chief memory of mother in my early years was my longing to live with her. This longing was never satisfied. My early photos show a pretty little girl, well dressed but sad looking, and I'm afraid they were accurate. Mother would re-appear from time to time but she never took me with her when she left.

One of the happiest parts of my early years was my mother's brother, Uncle Bert Glassey, who was very fond of me and who always brought me presents. He became a father substitute when we three moved to Raton, New Mexico, when I was about three. Uncle Bert worked on the Santa Fe Railroad and Grandmother kept house for him. We went to the Raton Baptist Church where I attended Sunday School. I learned to read even before starting school. My Grandmother was an avid reader of the Denver Post and she taught me to read the headlines. I also learned to read labels on cans and boxes.

I was a very feminine little girl who loved pretty dresses and pretty things. I liked to play with dolls and I heartily disliked and feared boys and their rough ways. As an only child I was not sure how to cope with them when they teased me. But I had some nice girl friends to play with - - - the three Mattox children and Mildred Andrews who lived in the neighborhood. They included me on family outings, climbing up the mountainside for a picnic. I thought it would be so wonderful to have a mother and dad, sisters and brothers. My grandmother was not too well and I'm afraid that as a child I did not appreciate her problems or like having to help around the house. And we never had enough money!

One of the things I hated the most was feeding the chickens, which Grandmother kept. They always seemed to get out of the fence and then I would have to chase them! One day I went into a cactus patch. The needles hurt my legs so I sat down. Grandma had to lay me over her lap and pull the needles out of my bottom. Worst of all, Uncle Bert watched and laughed!

In the fall of 1918, when I was 8, Grandma and I went to San Bernadino, California by train where my mother was. It took two days and two nights on the train.

It was exciting to eat on the train and at the Harvey House Restaurants. We lived there for a year but it was not a happy time. My mother's current partner was not suitable and ultimately we returned to Raton.

When I was ten years old, Uncle Bert married a nice young woman, Margaret Culp. The next year Grandmother died and I went to live with Uncle Bert and Aunt Margaret. I was very happy with them because Aunt Margaret was young, pretty and good to me. She taught me how to keep house and cook. She used to make Lady Baltimore cake, which I loved.

Soon she gave birth to a little boy, Eugene, who I enjoyed taking care of. At last I had a family and I also was finding high school fun. Because I was such a good student, the school moved me ahead a grade which was fine for the schoolwork but not for social-adjustment. However, by time I got to Junior High, I began to have more fun because the Baptist young people had many social activities. In eighth grade I was in the same class with Eugene Allbert whom I already knew from church Sunday school and Young People's Union.

We started dating in our sophomore year of high school.

The Allbert family invited me to join them on picnics. By the time we were juniors, we both thought we would eventually marry. At Raton High School I did well in

English and writing and I learned fast in the typewriting class, helping to type the Library book cards. Our school had so many exciting activities - - -not only sports teams but plays, orchestra and dances! At last I was accepted by many friends, doing well in school and busy with so many interesting activities. I loved my junior year of high school. These were the happiest days of my young life, soon to be sadly ended. I had formed many close friendships through the recently formed "Laff A Lot Club" which took on many responsibilities for school activities, such as selling football tickets; obtaining subscriptions for the year book ("The Black and Gold"); and planning for the Rally Day Dance. I was so proud to host the group in my Aunt's lovely home in May, 1925.

In November, 1925, we hosted the championship grid squad to a banquet and entertainment at the Methodist Church. After the banquet, the newspaper reported that "The Laff-a-Lot" girls gave one of the most enjoyable dances ever given in the Gym".

One of the happiest days of my life was April 15, 1926, the day of the District Typewriting contest. I had not planned on winning at all but it appears my fingers fairly flew and even though I beat the Dawson girl by seven-eighths of a word, it was at least a victory. All day my friends congratulated me and I was so proud and happy, not only because I had won for myself, but for my school.

Another day, which I shall never forget was the day when Ruth came up and told me her troubles about Robert and cried on my shoulder. Although my heart ached and I cried in sympathy with her, I was glad that she had enough confidence in me to tell me when she had told no one else. ["Days to be remembered" in Dorothy's Memory Book]

Then, in the spring of 1926, the bottom fell out of my world when I learned that my Aunt Margaret, Uncle Bert and little Gene were moving to Florida where he had bought some land. They were not taking me with them! Instead, I must move to Council Bluffs, Iowa, to live with my father and stepmother! This meant that I must leave, not only my beloved family, but my school, my boyfriend, Eugene, and all my friends. In my Memory Book, my dearest friends expressed their regrets that I would not be there for senior year and wished me well, saying nice things about my sweet disposition and brains. But nothing could really console me and I'm afraid I did not approach Council Bluffs with a positive attitude.

Council Bluffs was a mid-Western railroad center, a prosperous town but it was not home! I had not seen my father since I was a child and I had never met his wife, Marie, or their two children, a boy and a girl in their teens. I entered my senior year at the high school knowing no one, which everyone knows is a difficult challenge. I had my own room and I am sure that my father and stepmother tried to make me feel welcome but nonetheless, I did not. No doubt it was hard for them to take on another adolescent but I of course did not understand that point of view. I was only sixteen years old. I hated the long, bitterly cold winters.

I must have conveyed my misery in my letters to Eugene, for he stopped to see me on his way to East Pittsburgh the next summer. Our romance continued. After graduation from high school, I found a job with an insurance company as a secretary. Later, I found a better position as secretary to the manager of a wax manufacturing plant.

Probably my biggest reason for wanting to leave Council Bluffs was my father, whose affection toward me did not seem strictly paternal. So, when Eugene returned in 1929, once in June and again in August, I agreed to become engaged, with plans to marry the next year. In June 1930, I traveled to Turtle Creek, PA, to marry Eugene. I had been so unhappy most of my life to date that I was determined to make the future different.

CHAPTER II

GENE AND DOROTHY 1908-2000

Life in Turtle Creek, Pa, 1927-1947

EUGENE: (Autobiography and Essays)

In July of 1927 I left New Mexico to go to East Pittsburgh, Pennsylvania, where the Westinghouse Plant was located. After three weeks of visiting and riding, I looked out the window of the train and noticed a great number of dark, grey houses one room wide, two rooms long and from three to five stories high. This gave me the blues. This was August 5. I arrived at East Pittsburgh and came into the Educational Department. Mr. Brant asked me what he could do for me. I told him my story and showed him the letter which was sent to me. Mr. Brant told me Mr. Kettering was the man whom I desired to see and introduced me to him. I knew I was quite dirty from riding on the train but that didn't seem to make much difference to Mr. Kettering.

The Westinghouse Company plant was all you could see from the railroad station in East Pittsburgh. The Educational Department had its own building which I entered, along with others who were starting that day.

We were introduced around and given addresses where we might rent a room. We were told to return the next day at 7:00 a.m. and report for a shop assignment. Those in the Intermediate Course were paid $.33 per hour for the first six months and worked 48 hours a week. That was roughly $16 dollars a week!

I was given two addresses, one on Railroad Avenue in Turtle Creek and the other in Electric Plan on the hill. While the second was nicer, it cost more so I took the first. My room rent was $10.00 a month but after a little while I was able to persuade Eva and Albert Stranberg [the landlords] to give me board and room for $10.00 per week. Dorothy tells me Eva wasn't a very good cook, but I had enough to eat and only got worms once. I had left Raton with $125.00 and spent $65 on railroad fare. On August 13, I put $50.00 in the bank.

EDITOR

Gene began the practice of keeping detailed records of all expenditures in a little yearly account book, all of which he saved and which I have today.

EUGENE:

My first assignment was in section T-10 where coils were wound and stored for the Motor Department. The work was in the storeroom for a month, then testing coils for another month. We had four hours of classroom each week. Night school started in September. It was three hours a night, three days a week, so I was really busy. My shop training was complete by January, 1928 and I was assigned to the control drawing room in

February. This pleased me because I could perform quite well there. I made panel layout drawings for a short time and then started in the electrical diagram group. I could soon understand some of the circuitry, and with my classwork was able to make good progress. I was assigned to the control panel assembly section in the shop in April, 1929 for two weeks and then to control test for six weeks. This finished my course.

Two people who were good friends were Bartholomew J. Almone and a girl at church, Elizabeth Sanders. Bartholomew was an Italian, probably a Roman Catholic, who was in the student course with me. We took walks around East Pittsburgh and enjoyed talking. He was smart and was able to get a Lamme scholarship to go on to the University. He was my best man at my wedding. Elizabeth's home was on the hill near where I lived. We walked home from church affairs together. I told her about Dorothy when we first met in 1927 and explained my intention to marry Dorothy. I said I liked her company but she should not let our friendship limit her dating other men. She accompanied Dorothy at our wedding.

I had found the Baptist Church soon after arriving in Turtle Creek and went there the first Sunday. They greeted me with: "Where were you yesterday, we had a letter telling us you would be here. You would have enjoyed our church picnic". With this warm welcome and because I met many young men who were or had been in student courses, it was easy to get acquainted. It was not long before I became active in the Young People's Union and the Triangle Group in churches in Homestead, Turtle Creek and Pitcairn. [All three towns were suburbs of Pittsburgh]. Fred Hague was President of this activity and later I got the job. We had group picnics, rallies and later took part in the National B[aptist[Y[oung Peoples'] F[ellowship] Convention in 1934.

First Baptist Church
OF
TURTLE CREEK, PENNSYLVANIA
217 CHURCH STREET

In 1929 after finishing my course, I took a leave of absence for three months and went by train to Peoria, Illinois, where I met Mother, Dad, Kenneth and Vernon. We visited for a while with aunts, uncles and cousins. Dad had a skin cancer on his right temple and had been advised to go to Savannah, Missouri to a clinic where the cancer was removed by chemical burning. Dad and I left Peoria one morning at 3:00 a.m. in the 1929 Ford for

Savannah. I left him there and drove north to Council Bluffs to see Dorothy. We visited a couple days. I then drove back to Peoria.

Kenneth, Vernon, Mother and I drove to Kansas City to pick up Dad at Aunt Ida's and then drove to Raton by way of Lincoln, Nebraska, Denver and home. I had made arrangements to work for Tomlinson while home. I came back to East Pittsburgh by way of Council Bluffs. I proposed to Dorothy and she accepted. We set a time in September 1930 to be married. We continued our correspondence and in early 1930 a letter came stating that her company was going bankrupt. She suggested changing our wedding date to June when I would be out of night school. This was agreeable to me. I had told Mr. Tomlinson I would like to have him buy a ring for me when I was ready because I would get it from him at his cost. I ordered the engagement ring, which I sent to Dorothy around Easter time.

When I returned to Westinghouse, I was working as a regular draftsman, making and checking electrical diagram drawings. There was a need in the apprenticeship program for someone to teach the reading of electrical diagrams. I had done some of this while in the Intermediate Course, and was asked to continue. The Educational Department found I was a source of skilled labor and I worked overtime there on various paperwork jobs.

DOROTHY: (Autobiography and "Our Wedding Book")

Turtle Creek, Pennsylvania seemed a rather desolate place to a 20-year-old bride from Iowa.

The City of Council Bluffs, where I had lived for four years, was such a contrast to what I now, was beholding and where I would live indefinitely. Iowa was so lush and green with many trees, beautiful lawns, flower beds and pleasant homes. Turtle Creek by contrast seemed to have no lawns or flower beds and very few trees. The homes, though probably pleasant to the people who lived in them, seemed so strange to me. Almost all of them, though apparently built for one family, were occupied by two, and we found ourselves a part of that pattern.

Our Marriage [Book given to Gene and Dorothy by Pastor; Dorothy's hand written account]:

As our wedding, did not take place at the bride's home in Council Bluffs, Iowa, but at the groom's home in Turtle Creek, Pa., we had only a very simple ceremony performed at the home of Rev. A. A. Wainwright, 120 Sixth Street, Turtle Creek, Pastor of the First Baptist Church.

The wedding took place at 1:00 p.m. June 30th, 1930. The bride wore a chiffon dress of pink rose on a white back ground, a light horsehair braid hat, light shoes and hose and carried a bouquet of pink roses. She was attended by Miss Elizabeth Sanders, who wore a yellow chiffon dress and a light hat. Bart Almone ..... served the groom as best man.

Immediately after the ceremony Rev. & Mrs. Wainwright motored the bride and groom to Seidel's place at Conneaut Lake, Penna., where they spent a week's honeymoon. The bride's going away costume consisted of a blue flat crepe dress with a jacket and her wedding accessories. Mrs. Wainwright was our only guest beside our attendants.

Dorothy: (Autobiography)

We took a bus back to Turtle Creek. Many years later, our granddaughter, Cindy, asked us to fill out a form for her grammar school class, asking Grandparents about their early life. In response to the question: "What surprised you the most about your new spouse after you were married", Gene wrote: "That I finally had a pretty girl to live with, having been raised with brothers, the habits and whims of a woman seemed very strange."

Dorothy wrote: "Eugene's total devotion to his church and its activities."

The young people that Gene had boarded with [The Stranbergs] had moved from Railroad Avenue to George Street in the Electric Plan [on the hill]. They had made a housekeeping apartment of two of their bedrooms and it was there, after a week's honeymoon, that we set up housekeeping. There was another room on that floor that was rented out. Hud and Eva Stranberg and their two little boys lived in the three downstairs rooms, having converted the dining room into a bedroom. There was one bathroom for all and I carried the water I needed in the kitchen from the bathroom.

The summer weather was extremely hot and the absence of cool leafy trees made it hotter. There was always a haze in the air which was composed of soot and iron dust from the many factories in the area. This unpleasant ingredient in the air seemed to cover everything and it was black. Our nostrils were black from breathing it. The children were black in their play in an hour's time and to keep our homes clean from the black dust was a constant battle. As fall and winter came the haze became thicker and blacker as the houses and business places were heated with furnaces burning soft coal.

It was a surprise to me to find the people poorly educated. Many of them had emigrated, mostly from the British Isles and from southern Europe. The people from the Isles had little regard for the ones called foreigners.

The young people were mostly American born but had been influenced at home by the superstitions and strange ideas of their parents, many of whom did not speak English well, if at all. The people, though friendly, were very clannish. I was shocked frequently by their poor grammar. They used so many strange terms to me, like "poke" for a paper bag and "red up" for cleaning the house and "dear" for expensive. I'm afraid my lofty attitude was obvious which didn't help my popularity. So many of the younger people had left school at sixth or eighth grade and had gone to work for "The Westinghouse" or the steel mills and had contributed their wages at home until they were married.

We did have some good friends however, mostly at the Baptist Church. Some of these people we felt were on a level with us and some of these friendships lasted a lifetime.

EUGENE: (Autobiography)

I was permitted to go in the Graduate Student Program on November 1, 1930. There were six weeks of engineering school and a month on the motor test floor. The effects of the 1929 market crash were beginning to be felt and on February 16, 1931, I went back on drafting in the Control Engineering Department. Westinghouse closed the student programs. Most of the time that I was on motor test I worked nights. This made it nice for

Dorothy because she liked to sleep, and after serving me breakfast, she could come back to bed. We liked our third-floor apartment and managed to live there happily, although it was cold in the winter and hot in the summer.

EDITOR

The Stock Market Crash of 1929 had complex origins. The 1920s were years of excess for those fortunate enough to be wealthy---the so-called flapper generation, fueled by alcohol and jazz. But they became years of desperation for the farmers in the Middle West, who had borrowed to buy heavy equipment to meet the post-war demand for their products when the United States was supplying war-torn Europe with food. But when the demand for agricultural goods lessened, farmers found themselves unable to pay back their loans in an era of tight credit. And so, the banks foreclosed and many lost their farms. Meanwhile, the stock market was booming, with investors borrowing on low margin requirements. Finally, in 1929, the boom turned to bust; the stock market crashed. President Hoover proved unable to find a solution for the widespread depression which followed. It was in these desperate economic circumstances that Franklin Delano Roosevelt was elected President in 1932, as the first Democratic President since Woodrow Wilson.

EUGENE: (Autobiography)

Westinghouse continued to feel the pinch of the Depression. Layoffs took place in all departments. Our diagram group lost two-thirds of its men.

Those draftsmen remaining had a 10 per cent cut in salary and worked only three weeks a month. Some rush jobs required overtime. For this we received a 65-cent meal ticket to be used at the company cafeteria. I walked to work and to church.

Dorothy became pregnant in the summer of 1932. We had moved from a third-floor apartment, 520 James Street, to a fourth floor of the second house, 518 James Street, that Cupaks owned, to reduce our rent to $15 per month for three rooms and a bath. Margaret Louise was born on March 5, 1933. She was a lovely baby and we were very happy. Franklin D. Roosevelt was inaugurated on March 4 and he closed all the banks on the 5th. Our money to pay the hospital was in the bank and this bill did not get paid for a year when some funds were released.

One of our friends, Gladys Stewart, was a schoolteacher. She wanted to take an automobile trip west and asked if we would like to go to see my parents in Raton, New Mexico. She said she would furnish the car if we would furnish the money. Margaret was only five months old and we thought we could handle feeding, using canned milk and distilled water. The doctor thought it was o.k. I talked to Mr. Bogarts, my boss's boss, and he said he would give me the days. I had worked overtime to extend my vacation beyond the two weeks allowed.

 Gladys had a Pontiac sedan. We had $85 and a 5-month old baby. Our first stop was to be somewhere in Chicago. At lunchtime, we were in Ohio and had installed one new radiator hose. The temperature was 110 F. We did not get to our destination until about midnight. The next day Dorothy and Margaret rested and Gladys and I went to the 1933 World's Fair. Our next stop was with my relatives in Peoria, Illinois, not a long trip. We were welcomed and made over, especially Peggy. The next stop was near Council Bluffs, Iowa, Dorothy's father's home. While in Council Bluffs, we bought a new tire and had the front end of the car aligned.

 Peggy was doing well. Her food, canned milk and distilled water, worked fine and we had learned to hold diapers out the window to dry them. We stopped in Dodge City, Kansas and slept in a cabin the last night before we came to Raton. The cabin was hot but they had a shower house and we slept well. Gladys drove over the Raton Pass at night. She could not see the drop-off along the road, so was not frightened. I was too sleepy to drive. We enjoyed our visit with my parents and brothers and they of course enjoyed meeting their granddaughter. Dad had to add twenty-five dollars to help us on the way home.

In early 1934 we moved to a second-floor apartment for $20 per month---four rooms and a bath. The Depression began to ease some. Prices were still low---bread $.10 a loaf; peanut butter $.10 a pound; and a White Tower hamburger $.05. Dorothy became pregnant again and very much so.

In the early morning of February 11, 1935, Dorothy said: "It is time".

I called Dr. Morton and told him that I was taking Dorothy to the Wilkinsburg Hospital. Sometime after this Dorothy presented him with a baby girl and he told her there was another baby in there almost ready to be born. Soon there were two baby girls exercising their lungs. Dr. Morton greeted me with the news that I was the father of twin daughters. I went to see Dorothy and we talked about our new adventure. Our older daughter, Margaret, would be two on March 5th. We decided to keep both of the twins, even though friends of ours would have been happy to have one. We named the twins Ruth and Roberta. Mother was in Peoria on her way to see us. Mr. and Mrs. Ray and Treva Grimes, friends of ours, helped until Mother arrived.

EDITOR

My sisters and I were shocked to learn that Mom and Dad even had considered giving one of the twins away! It was a well-guarded family secret which was a good indication of their poverty at that time.

EUGENE: (Autobiography)

Everyone seemed to be excited about the twins. That part was fine. But soon we were working hard to keep up with their needs. My part was the washing. I remember hanging out 57 diapers at one time. Mother stayed for six weeks and most things were under control. We bought a wicker twin baby buggy from acquaintances, which fit through the door and there was space in the hallway to keep it when not in use. The children were sick when they were two months old. Peggy recovered soon, next Ruth, but Roberta had a bronchial cough for about two months. In the summer, it was very hot in our apartment and our babies were suffering from the heat. Dorothy took a block of ice out of the ice box, set it in a dish pan, and used the fan to blow air over it to cool our babies and herself. This was an extreme measure I thought but it worked!

When the twins started to walk, and run around the apartment, Cupaks, our landlords, thought we should look for a house. We were slow about this but we were glad we were still on the hill area called the Electric Plan in the winter of 1935-36---after a cold winter, the snow and ice did not melt before the rains came in March. On the 17th the rivers backed up and all the valleys were flooded. Pittsburgh had about 1 ½ stories of water and the power plants were inundated so there was no electricity for three or four days. We had water and gas. We boiled our water.

The Westinghouse plant had about 16 feet of water on the main manufacturing floor. Westinghouse stored all their drawings on the first floor and these got wet. These were the records of all their engineering work; it was before microfiche. Drawings were made on linen tracings with India ink. The new process had been used on some, which had a photosensitive film on the linen. We were asked to come into the plant and hang up the drawings to save as many as possible. The inked drawings came through quite well. The others had to be retraced.

Dad and Mother thought it would be a good thing for Dorothy and the children to spend a summer in New Mexico. In July, they went by train to New Mexico. For Dorothy, it was a difficult two days and nights on the train, but they were warmly greeted by the loving grandparents in Gardiner. I was to find a house for us to move into when the family returned.

EDITOR

Dorothy hand wrote on this section in 1999:

"One of the greatest mistakes of my life!" I suspect she was remembering how difficult it had been, both to travel alone with three babies, and to live with her mother-in-law.

EUGENE: (Autobiography)

In September 1936, I found a five-room house to rent for $25 per month. In early October, our family was together again. We had enough furniture for three rooms and spread it out over five. There was a lot of space for the children to run and play. To get the house for $25 per month, I had agreed to re-putty the windows, sand the floors and refinish them and do any painting required. I learned later that the mortgage payment on the house was $33 per month. The walk to church was on the level and we all walked. We bought dining room furniture which had been in storage; a table, six chairs, buffet and china closet for $35. Now we did not have the money, so a friend loaned us $30 on the basis that we pay it back in six months. To get living room furniture we bought it on time---$10 down and $10 per month.

Our house on Sixth Street had a basement door that opened onto a vacant lot, part of which was lower than the basement level. The children liked to play in the basement and in this yard. For several Christmas seasons, the lot across Sixth Street served as a Christmas tree lot. The children spent a lot of time running around among the trees.

EDITOR

I always will remember playing in the Christmas Tree lot, where we built igloos and played for hours. The fragrance of the pine boughs was wonderful!

EUGENE: (Autobiography and essay, 11/6/95)

By 1937 we were beginning to come out of the Depression and Westinghouse started their apprentice program again. I was asked to teach the apprentices how to read wiring diagrams. This was during working hours and didn't increase my pay but I had had raises. I told my landlord that I could increase my rent to $30 per month. I think the Westinghouse Credit Union was started about 1937. I was active in it and have number 42 as my account number. I served one year as President of the

Union. The Social Security System started and we noticed the first deduction from our checks.

We had formed many good friends among the church members: Rhoda and Clifford Allen; Ethel and George Richard; Ruth and Red O'Conner and Gladys Stewart. My work with the young people of the Triangle Group gave me contact with people from the Pitcairn and Homestead churches. Mr. and Mrs. Hague and Mr. and Mrs. Chuska became friends of ours. The summer of 1939 the Chuskas and their son took us up to Lake Erie for a week's vacation. While we were there, World War II began in Europe.

EDITOR

World War II began in Europe in September 1939, when Hitler's German troops invaded Poland. Poland's independence had been guaranteed by Great Britain and France after the first World War. Reluctantly, the two countries declared war on Germany, recognizing that the doctrine of appeasement would not stop Nazi aggression in Europe. This time, the American people were determined to stay out of the war, despite their sympathy for the British. But on December 7, 1941, the Japanese, who had allied with Germany, attacked Pearl Harbor, the huge American naval base in Hawaii, killing thousands and destroying a good portion of the U.S.

Pacific fleet. Only then did President Roosevelt declare war on Japan, Germany and the Axis Powers.

EUGENE: (Autobiography)

That same summer [1939] a new girl came to play with the twins. She was Roberta Robinson who was six months younger. That evening her parents, Betty and Al Robinson, came to our house to check on the new friends their daughter had made. This ripened into an excellent friendship. Al was a parts man at the Ford garage and since he had a car, we decided we could afford a car and bought a used Dodge in 1940: a 1936 green sedan. Dorothy said that we were so happy because we had been without a car all of our married life.

DOROTHY: (Autobiography)

I do not think I could have made it through the long war years without Betty's friendship. We enjoyed talking by the hour and an occasional movie. She and Bobbie went to Sunday School and Church with us. Al and Gene were congenial too and our two families had many happy times together

EUGENE: (Autobiography)

We were feeling more prosperous by this time so we went to Fineman's, [a Department Store] to buy me a new suit. One was selected, a dark green for $39, and Mr. Fineman told us he had another suit in my size and if I wanted it I could have it for $11. It was a sharkskin weave in a tweedy grey color. We took them both. I don't remember ever wearing out the sharkskin suit. It lasted a long time.

DOROTHY (Autobiography)

Our lives all changed after December 7, 1941 when Pearl Harbor was bombed and war with Japan was declared. Turtle Creek was dirtier than ever because of the war effort. World War II was a sad time--- so many young men kept leaving, some never to return. Rationing and shortages were a continuing fact of life and anxiety over the bad news from the Pacific and Europe haunted our days and nights. Although Gene was in the draft age group, he was given deferments because his work at Westinghouse was essential. Beside this he taught Defense School three nights a week.

EUGENE: (Autobiography)

I taught Wiring Diagram Reading. The plant organized a Defense Warden system. I was assigned a group of men to train and an area of the plant roofs and yards for these men to patrol in case of an attack. Some of our wiring diagrams were now made for submarine controls instead of steel mills. At home, we had blackout curtains for our windows and it wasn't long until rationing was introduced. We did not use our car much because of the gasoline rationing. Soon we sold it to one of the church members who needed it to go to work. He could get gasoline. Otherwise, things went on as usual except for scarce butter and nylon stockings.

In 1944, the Roneys [neighbors] put their house on the market but told us first so we could buy it. They also agreed to a second mortgage. They wanted $5,200 for 113 Sixth Street, one of the houses Westinghouse had built in the area about 20 years before. We sold our war bonds and were able to make a down payment. We moved almost all of our belongings across the street except the heavy pieces. George Bishop [a church friend] moved those for us.

Our house had a large kitchen that had been built on the house. Dorothy found it very inefficient. One of the bedrooms upstairs had been divided into two rooms. We decided to take that partition out and put it into the kitchen, taking about one quarter for storage. The three-fourths left would be much easier to use, less distance to the refrigerator and cabinets. The change worked well.

In 1944, Engineer Willard Cook resigned. I was promoted to the engineer position. An early design job was for a mine hoist. This was a DC drive and something I could get through okay. It went into operation satisfactorily in Carlsbad, New Mexico. A new regulator, called a Rototrol, had been shipped to Armco Steel at Middletown, Ohio and was ready for field testing. I was sent out with one of the Motor Division engineers to determine how it would work. The Armco engineer was very helpful and we found the Rototrol was able to control the strip tension on the reel of a three-stand cold roll mill.

One evening while working at this Mill, we went out to dinner and discussed the possibility of the end of war with Japan. [The European War had ended on May 8, 1945.] The Armco engineer said he thought the mill people would keep on working if the war ended. Just then, a policeman opened the restaurant door and said to lock the door. The War was over!

All the whistles in the mill began to blow and the street was filled with people. We went back to the mill and released the whistles, then shut down equipment. Our serviceman said he would see us in a couple of days and left. August 14, 1945, was a great day! It also celebrated Dorothy's 35th birthday. She said the streets of Turtle Creek and East Pittsburgh were full of happy people.

DOROTHY: (Autobiography)

Everyone was happy and relieved that the long and terrible war was finally concluded. There were still hardships on the home front. Our family life continued happily. The girls were all in grade school now. They were good students and took part in any activity that came along. They were active in Sunday School and Church too and all had been baptized. We were all increasingly busy.

Gene was frequently absent with Westinghouse business and the girls with their school and I was homeroom mother every year, which was a pleasant change from housework. The girls learned to sing in a children's chorus at church. They had an able instructor in Mrs. Nagel, a former teacher and music instructor. Ruth had longed to start music with piano lessons, which she finally did. Peggy had three years of piano lessons but tired of it. Roberta never found time to take lessons.

EDITOR

Mrs. Nagle taught my sisters and I to sing three-part harmony, which we did in many future performances. She was a remarkable music teacher.

EUGENE: (Autobiography)

As an engineer, one of my next jobs was to design the control equipment for a reversing cold mill, then known as a Sendzirir mill. The district office engineer had prepared a specification in some detail on how the design should be made. I did not like what was proposed and thought I had a better plan. The order stayed on my desk for some time before I decided to go my own way; not follow what Mr. Cook [had suggested] and not follow the specification. As I look back on it now, it was a rash decision, but the results were excellent. The mill builder's engineer said it was the best controlled mill he had installed. Twenty-five years later I went to see the mill. The control panel looked just like we had left it and the coil size had been doubled. This would have put the specified control out of range.

A strike by the plant CIO workers was called in the fall of 1945. I had planned a trip to Armco, taking along an Esterline Argus recording ammeter. So, I got on the train for Middletown and did my work there. When finished, I took a train back and found our engineers working in a former shoe store in Squirrel Hill [a nearby neighborhood]. We worked in this office until the spring of 1946.

The Motor Division of Westinghouse needed more space. The Curtiss-Wright plant in Buffalo, New York, was selected for their move and in 1946 they started to leave East Pittsburgh. The Control Division started to move in 1947 and I was transferred there on August 1.

Dorothy: (Autobiography)

This news was received by our family with mixed emotion. Life in Turtle Creek seemed very good to us at that point. Our friends at the Baptist Church also seemed to regret our leaving. Gene had always been so active there and I had some responsibilities, too. The Church had a nice party for us and the Ellises, who were moving to Beaver, Pennsylvania. The Church gave us both beautiful lace tablecloths as parting gifts.

The housing situation had been a source of worry but was solved for us almost providentially it seemed. The house we had owned for only three years was sold to a couple from the church who called and asked to buy it. Gene had seen a house when he was in Buffalo on business that two of the Motor men had recommended. So in March, I went up to see it and the middle of April we closed the deal. In late May, 1947, the girls and I moved to Buffalo. Gene's work was not transferred until August.

During the summer Gene boarded with the Robinsons and came home most weekends.

We were all delighted with our new home. It had been recently redecorated and was perfectly clean. There were beautiful hardwood floors and oak woodwork downstairs. Our furniture was pretty shabby, as during the long war years, new furniture was not available. So soon I set out to remedy this matter. We bought new living and dining room furniture; a new rug for the living room and new kitchen range.

EUGENE: (Autobiography)

The early part of June, 1947, I was told the International Mineral and Chemical Company would not pay all of the money for the mine hoist until an engineer came down and discussed the control with their engineers. It was my design so I went to Carlsbad, [New Mexico] and met with a group to tell how the control operated and the functions of each major piece. I hadn't gone very far talking about the equipment before a man left the room and I was told the meeting was over. Apparently, there was a question of why we had used a slip regulator. When the person had the answer, he paid the remainder of the bill.

While in Carlsbad they took me into the mine 900 feet deep where they obtained potash. Then I went through the Carlsbad Caverns and decided to take some vacation. I took a bus to Raton and visited Mother and Dad. Mother suggested we go to see Kenneth in Cortez, Colorado. The two of us drove to Walsenburg, then west across southern Colorado to Cortez. I think we stayed only one day and returned. To get a plane to Pittsburgh I had to go to Albuquerque by bus. It had been an interesting trip and vacation.

CHAPTER III

GENE AND DOROTHY: 1908-2000

Buffalo, New York, 1947-1957:

Expanding Horizons

EDITOR

Dorothy began keeping a diary in 1948; skipped '49 and '50, and kept limited entries for '51-'53. The diaries for '55, '56 and '57 provide very full accounts of the Allberts' family life. To vividly and accurately convey Dorothy's perception of these days, I have quoted these diaries directly, choosing those comments which most typically express her feelings. Most of these events relate to the trials of motherhood: The challenges of raising three teen-age daughters. All of course, affected Gene and Dorothy's marriage.

The move from Turtle Creek, PA, to Buffalo, NY in 1947 represented a significant change in Gene and Dorothy's lives and in that of their daughters as well. The relocation came at an ideal moment for both generations---the parents still were young enough to change and grow: the children were in the early, formative stage of adolescence.

In 1947, Buffalo was a major American industrial city, still benefitting from the industrial demands of World War II, and the postwar economic boom, caused by the need to supply war ravaged Europe. North Buffalo, where the Allberts bought a home, was close to both the University of Buffalo and to most of Buffalo's rich cultural sites, such as the Albright Art Gallery; the Historical Museum and Kleinhans Music Hall. Therefore, many well-educated people chose to live in this area.

Buffalo was an ethnic community, characterized by Irish living in South Buffalo, Italians on the West Side and Polish on the East Side. African Americans in large numbers had emigrated from the South during World War II, settling on the East Side. North Buffalo included a large Jewish population as well as a diverse mixture of other nationalities. Thus, when the Allbert girls entered school #63 and Bennett High School, (the twins in 7th grade and Peggy a Freshman), they encountered for the first time, people from a much wider spectrum of American society than they previously had known.

Jim and Eva Ball were a family who befriended the Allberts that summer. They lived nearby and they had two daughters, Ruth and Barbara, who were about the same age as the twins. The Balls invited the Allberts to attend the Delavan Avenue Baptist Church with them and shortly thereafter, Gene and Dorothy decided to become members. Delavan Avenue belonged to the American Baptist Convention, an organization far more liberal than the Southern Baptist churches in Raton and Turtle Creek. Nonetheless, church membership still involved two services on Sunday, prayer meeting on Wednesday, and weekly Young Peoples' meetings.

From childhood, Eugene and Dorothy had been taught that drinking alcoholic beverages, playing cards and dancing were immoral; as was going to the movies on Sunday. But the people of Delavan Avenue had a much more relaxed attitude towards such activities. Soon Dorothy found herself playing pinochle (a card game) at Missionary Society! While shocked, she enjoyed it! The girls quickly learned to dance, an activity which became an important part of their social life at Bennett High School.

And so, Gene and Dorothy began to change with the times. However, when Grandma and Grandpa Allbert came to visit from New Mexico, the cards were hidden away and dancing was not discussed. Nor were alcoholic beverages ever served in the Allbert home. Furthermore, the grandparents were shocked to find that Buffalo was largely a Catholic community. When visiting, Grandpa Allbert regularly walked over to Bailey Avenue (the business district) to try to convert Catholic people! At Delavan Avenue, Gene and Dorothy formed many wonderful friendships and enjoyed a very active social life.

In addition to their new church friends, Gene and Dorothy became friends with many Westinghouse people who also had been transferred to Buffalo from Pittsburgh. Most important of these were Jim and Mary Love, who lived down the street from them on La Salle Avenue, and the Abells, who lived next door. Dorothy and Mary Love were to spend many hours together over the next few years.

EUGENE: (Autobiography and essays)

The steel mill workload was increasing and Mr. F. M. Parks was going to retire in 1950. Mr. Markle, the

Manager of our Engineering Department, asked me to be the Section Engineer of the Heavy Mill Section. I accepted this [assignment] and my design days were over, but not the responsibility. Orders for steel mill equipment increased. New engineers were hired. Many came from the Navy and its V-12 programs. Everybody had held some sort of responsible positions, so it was easy for me to make assignments to them. I found it necessary to write instructions on what line of apparatus should be used so that we would get uniform looking control panels. In making my assignments I told them they would be responsible for: the design, for following it through the drawing room, the shop and test and finally, if necessary, for adjusting it in the customer's plant to his satisfaction. I would try to answer any of their questions.

 The electrical drives for steel mill equipment were in great demand and my section had been assigned four of the better engineers to supervise the various kinds of control equipment we designed. The orders for steel mill controls continued to increase from 1957. The engineers in my section could not handle the work so engineers from the District were brought in to help. Then the drafting room could no longer do all the work and some was farmed out to Canadian Westinghouse. Mr. Dan Pierce negotiated this and one of the Canadian engineers was the contact person. Auburn Associates in Pittsburgh also made drawings for us and I made the contacts there. As I remember it, I flew down in the evening and stayed at a motel in Monroeville [the suburb where the Robinsons lived]. I made an 8 a.m. visit to the Forest

Hills Office of Auburn Associates and ate lunch on my way to a second office in South Side Pittsburgh. When I had finished my work there, I drove to the airport and took a plane back to Buffalo. This occurred two times a week for a while. Also during this time, magnetic amplifiers (a saturable core reactor) were developed and used in place of the Rototrol. Because of the unpredictable characteristics of these, there were many problems.

EDITOR

Beginning in 1946, and continuing into the 1960s, Eugene was awarded 12 patents for inventions he made at Westinghouse. Although these patents belonged to Westinghouse, and Gene did not profit significantly (he received $50.00 per patent), one assumes his inventions increased his standing with the company. The young engineers whom Gene supervised, gradually became good friends since he took a personal interest in all of them. They all were college graduates who rose quickly at Westinghouse, ultimately outranking Gene and becoming his supervisor. However, the close relationships formed with men like Don Abel, Bill Roberts and Jerry Mathias, continued the rest of their lives. At his retirement dinner one of his associates joked about Gene's keeping track of every penny spent on business trips. When Gene received his 30 year service pin from Westinghouse, an article reviewed Gene's career to date and commented: "It has been said that the years Gene spent in the various shop sections partially explain his ability to accept a telephone call for miscellaneous parts required on a field trouble job and have them on a plane an hour or two later."

With Gene being so busy at work and traveling on business trips, most of the home responsibilities fell on Dorothy's shoulders. Her diaries suggest how difficult these responsibilities were for her.

Dorothy: (Diary)

<u>1948</u>

February 11: This is the twin's birthday and they are <u>13</u>! It doesn't seem possible! They are such grand girls!

Feb. 18: I hate to think how much of my life I have spent at the ironing board.

Feb. 21: I like to keep house and am thrilled at having such a nice place to keep. It is nicer than I had ever expected to have.

Feb. 24: I enjoy the fellowship of the [Delavan church] people there so much. They are so nice to us!

March 1: To Turtle Creek: Bette [Robinson] and I are so glad to see each other and have so much to say it will probably take most of the night.

March 6: I like the Delavan Avenue Church better than the Turtle Creek one.

March 8: Everything here is so much pleasanter than dirty old Turtle Creek was.

March 11: So much of my time goes to my family's stomachs.

March 24: I cleaned the wallpaper in the living room. Tonight, we went for a little ride in <u>our new car.</u>

March 25: I wish I knew some way to regulate the amount of company the girls have.

April 5: I hung the sheets, towels, socks and undies outside and they dried nicely.

April 19: I feel like I could spend the rest of my life in bed!

April 20: The twins are to sing at an Assembly next month.

April 28: Gene was elected a Deacon and they want him to be Superintendent of Sunday School.

May 4: I washed the lower part of the kitchen walls so Gene can paint them tonight.

May 8: What a lift it gives me to get something new for the house.

May 13: There is <u>never</u> enough money!

May 27: What a job to keep three teen age girls dressed!

May 31: I'll never have another friend like Bette, I know.

June 3: Bobbi Robinson [who was visiting] went to school with the twins yesterday. She is such a nice child.

EDITOR

Another Buffalo tradition was for families to own a summer cottage at the beach, either on the American or Canadian side of Lake Erie, and/or a cabin in the country. Such ownership did not necessarily reflect great wealth, since often these vacation sites were very simple and had been inherited. For example, Jim Ball, who was a school teacher, owned both a farm south of Buffalo and a cabin in Canada.

DOROTHY: (Diary)

June 5: Ball's farm: The farm is nice and the girls are having the time of their lives. There are 13 girls, the Balls and us and Ellis Ball who lives here. We served dinner and supper cafeteria style and how those kids can put away food! We cook and the girls do dishes. It is really beautiful here but there is so much confusion!

June 10: I always feel guilty when I let a whole day go by without doing any work.

June 24: Tonight we heard Mr. Dewey's acceptance speech [as the Republican Nominee for President]. Radio is such a marvelous thing.

EDITOR

The Presidential election of 1948 was one of the most surprising political events in American history, since everyone assumed that the Republican Candidate, Thomas E. Dewey, would easily defeat the Democratic nominee, Harry S. Truman. Vice President Truman became President in April, 1945 when Franklin Roosevelt died, after serving only a few months of his unprecedented 4th term. Truman was totally unprepared, since he had not been informed on the great issues he faced in ending the war. Truman was not highly regarded by the American public. In fact, the newspapers already had printed the headlines of Dewey's victory! However, in 1948, the unimpressive Truman surprised the world by defeating Dewey.

These postwar years were a time of great uncertainty and fear, as Joseph Stalin, the dictator of the Soviet Union and a former American ally, expanded his control over Eastern Europe. Furthermore, the much hated communism seemed to be spreading around the globe, as the Chinese Communists expelled the American supported Chiang Kai-shek's Chinese Nationalists troops to the island of Formosa (Taiwan) in 1947 and proceeded to take control of mainland China.

In addition, the Soviet Union became a nuclear power. And so, the so-called "Cold War" began, with the two nuclear giants threatening each other with mutual destructions. The Cold War did not end until 1989!

While Gene and Dorothy closely followed these political events and regularly discussed them at the kitchen table, they never became actively involved in politics. They remained loyal Republicans. In the Presidential election of 1952, they voted for General Dwight D. Eisenhower, the Supreme Commander of World War II, hoping that his leadership would bring an end to the Korean War and the rabid McCarthyism which had swept the nation. In November, 1952, Eisenhower succeeded in ending Democratic control in Washington, D.C.

THIS IS THE WAY WE DRIE OUR CLOTHES

DOROTHY: (Autobiography):

On July 10, 1948, we left for Raton, New Mexico to visit Gene's folks. On the way, out we stopped at Aunt Sadie's in Peoria, Illinois, for a nice visit and then went on to Council Bluffs, Iowa, to see my folks. From there to Topeka, Kansas, where we stayed with Gene's brother, Vernon, and his wife, Charlotte. They are living in a state of armed neutrality! We were not sorry to leave. We pulled into Raton while the folks were having lunch and surprised them.

DOROTHY: (Diary)

July 19: The days always begin early at Mother Allbert's house! We were washing before eight o'clock. We sure had a big one too! Tonight, we took a ride around town. The girls were much interested in seeing the adobe houses the Mexicans live in and also in the entirely different types of architecture here from what they are used to in the East.

July 22: Mrs. Culp and the family visited Aunt Margaret's grave in Trinidad. [Dorothy's Uncle Bert's wife had died shortly after they moved to Florida. Mrs. Culp was Margaret's mother.] Edna Culp gave me some photographs of mine that were stored in their house for years and some dishes of my Aunt's and my grandmother's.

July 24: It is beautiful country out here but I wouldn't want to live out here again.

EDITOR

The high school years were very happy ones for the girls, since they were good students and very involved in many activities both at school and at church.

Gene and Dorothy opened their home to all their daughters' friends and Gene spent many hours, driving his daughters to club and sorority meetings, babysitting jobs, and in the summer, to Sherkston Beach (in Canada) and to Sunset Beach on the Lake Erie shore. All the girls learned to drive and finally, in 1954, Dorothy began driving.

She wrote: "The ability to drive enlarged my world beyond belief".

Although Peggy was very bright, she had not been as disciplined a student as her parents expected, so rather than sending her to University, they decided that she should go to Bryant and Stratton Business School. It was a decision which Gene and Dorothy deeply regretted in later years. When the twins graduated from Bennett in 1953, Ruthie decided to go to the local State Teacher's

College, while Roberta decided to attend the University of Rochester, which was sixty miles away. And so the twins were separated for the first time since birth.

During the high school and college years, Dorothy lived through many romances and emotional crises before her three daughters finally found the right man to marry: First, Peggy broke her engagement to Tommy Graham; then Ruth broke up with Dick Anthony; and finally, Roberta broke up with Roger Dayer. Since Dorothy had been very fond of all three young men; she suffered through each episode.

DOROTHY: (Diary)

1951

Feb. 4: Worked on church books all afternoon and most of the evening. [Dorothy was the unpaid Financial Secretary of Delavan Ave. Church.]

Mar. 6: Today about twelve of us went down to house-clean the church. The janitor is just plain lazy and the church has gotten so dirty we are ashamed of it.

Mar. 14: My family all treat me like I was something to wipe their feet on.

Mar. 28: Talked to E[dith] Smith [a church friend] over an hour on telephone.

April 24: Missionary Society installation of officers and I am President. Everyone was so nice I can't help being thrilled but it is sure a big job.

May 10: Don't know when I'll ever do Spring Cleaning.

May 12: Peggy was elected queen of Bryant & Stratton. So thrilled!

June 11: [Baptist] Convention! I was at Delaware Ave. church all day ushering for the Women's meeting. Nice but I'm so tired.

June 20: Twins doing their own ironing.

July 16: To Keuka College for Baptist Conference.

July 19: The people here are all so nice.

EDITOR

One of the highlights of the Allbert family life was their trip to New Mexico in August, 1954, for the grandparents' 50th anniversary. Much later Eugene wrote an essay describing the celebration.

EUGENE: (Essay written 2/27/1990)

My parents, Mr. and Mrs. Alva Allbert, had looked forward to their fiftieth wedding anniversary for the last year. They had been married in Raton, New Mexico, on August 28, 1904. Saturday, August 28, 1954, was the date for our party. Mother's sister, Margy, and niece, Mildred, came from Peoria, Illinois by train to start making preparations. Mother's sister, Sadie, rode with Eugene, his wife Dorothy, and their twin daughters, Ruth and Roberta. They drove from Buffalo, New York. The next day, son Kenneth arrived from Imperial, Nebraska and son Vernon came from Topeka, Kansas. Granddaughter Margaret was delayed by her work and flew in from Buffalo on a DC-3 plane that landed on the prairie south of town.

    The August weather was beautiful with New Mexico blue skies and the temperature around 80 degrees. It was time for Rockyford cantaloupe; someone purchased a case, we all enjoyed the delicious melon. 702 South Sixth Street buzzed with activity. One day, Ruth, Roberta, Vernon and Eugene drove to the coalmining town of Gardiner, three miles from Raton, where we once lived. We hiked up the mountain to a cave where the men had played years before. We could see the many changes in the town since the mines had closed. The frame houses had been sold and the adobe ones leveled. The next day the four of us, and Dorothy walked to Toad Stool Park. It was on top of one of the foothills of the Sangre de Christo range. Ruth and Roberta only went part way (the altitude was too high for them). They had not grown up in this area. The "toad stools" were round pedestals of off white sand stone with round, flat tops that overhung the pedestals.

    Saturday, we dressed in our best clothes for the party; took pictures and went to the First Baptist Church where the celebration would be. The Parlor was decorated for the occasion with the cake on the table in front. No others were there who remembered the wedding. Margaret, Ruth, Roberta and Vernon sang as part of the program. Dad gave a talk, the cake was cut and best wishes were given by all present. The peak of the celebration was over.

    Sunday, Kenneth and Margaret went home. Monday, Vernon started for Topeka. That afternoon, Dad, who had lived to enjoy his anniversary, had a heart attack and died the next day. It was a sad experience for all of us. But for him, he had lived a full and successful life. He had celebrated his fiftieth anniversary and I'm sure he felt his time had come. He was prepared to meet his maker.

EDITOR

A new problem developed after Grandpa's death, since it soon became clear that Grandma could not manage living alone. At first she divided her time between visiting Gene and Dorothy in Buffalo and her sisters in Peoria. The visits to Buffalo always were difficult for Dorothy, since Grandma believed that Monday was wash day, Tuesday for ironing, etc., while Dorothy followed a more flexible schedule. Dorothy confided to her diary: "I can do so much better when she isn't watching every move I make."

Dorothy still was overwhelmed with household chores and responsibilities involved with raising her daughters, although her new automatic washing machine helped to lighten the load. More and more she began to resent the constant demands of family and church. She wrote that she spent her life "doing for others". She also resented the time Gene spent on church activities and his reluctance to ever spend an evening at home.

An ongoing problem with which Dorothy struggled was weight and low blood pressure. She never possessed the energy or drive which her husband and mother-in-law enjoyed and thus found it difficult to live with their constant need to be working. She wrote on June 7, 1955: "My whole family is so demanding & unconcerned about my feelings."

DOROTHY: (Diary)

<u>1955</u>

Jan. 11: This has certainly been a busy day. I drove Ruth to school [Buffalo State College] this morning for her ten o'clock class, then came home and baked two apple pies for the church dinner tonight. Mother ironed until lunchtime and did all the ironing except five pieces. I went down to the church early this afternoon to help get the tables set and things ready for tonight. We are going to need every bit of table space we have to serve the crowd as people are still calling in reservations. I took some of my own dishes and silver down to make a few more places. I came home but only had a few minutes to rest and then cleaned up and back down to church. The dinner was a howling success financially as we made over $100 but we sure worked hard.

Jan. 12: I sure haven't done very much work today as I am very tired from such a big day yesterday. I did count the church money and got it ready to go to the bank and that is a job that has to be done every week so I always feel like I've accomplished something when that is done and the book posted.

Jan. 14: I just despise mending for some reason and always neglect it as long as possible.

Jan. 18: Mother left for home early this morning. I got up and got breakfast and Gene and I took her to the train. I tried to keep from showing it but I was so glad to have her leave. I just felt like I couldn't put up with her bossiness and criticisms another day.

Feb. 11: Today is our darling twins 20th birthday. It doesn't seem possible that they are grown women already. They have been a double blessing to us all their lives. When they were born we hardly knew how we could provide for them but the Lord has been so good to us that we have been able to raise them nice and give them good educations and we are very thankful for it all and especially for them.

March 5: Peggy's 22nd birthday! I was so thrilled with her when she was born and I am glad I have been lucky enough to have her at home this long.

March 10: Tonight Gene and I both had to go to an Officers meeting at church. It turned out to be one of those wrangly meetings and I got so upset. I can't stand fighting and disputing and I don't think church meetings should be that way.

March 16: Finished the ironing and washed the living room windows and put up freshly cleaned drapes. Gene stayed out to work until after ten tonight. He didn't even come home for dinner. I went to Prayer Meeting alone.

EDITOR

The celebration of the Allberts' 25th wedding anniversary provided Dorothy with a much-needed break from routine work.

Dorothy: (Diary)

1955

June 30: Our Silver Wedding Anniversary! And it has really been a Day of Days. I was given the whole day off & the girls & Chris [Vector, a friend from Turtle Creek who made beautiful cakes] did all the work for the party. This morning I went to the Beauty Parlor & had my hair cut, washed & set & my nails done. Gene came home at noon & took me out to the Cloud Room at the Air Port for lunch & then bought me a new wedding ring with five small diamonds in it.

    This evening all ten of us went to Lyons Tea Room for a lovely dinner & then from 8:00 we held "Open House". Over 100 of our friends came to congratulate us. Chris had a beautiful table set at the end of the Dining Room with the beautiful cake she baked; lovely fancy sandwiches; Punch, mints & nuts. The people almost all went down cellar to see our movies & slides & seemed to enjoy them a lot. We were just happy & thrilled beyond words with the whole occasion. We received many beautiful gifts too and announced Peg & John [Clarke]'s engagement.

July 1: Yesterday was one of the most wonderful days I have ever had. The wedding cake was so huge I knew we could never eat it before it got stale so I cut up the whole bottom layer into small pieces and made up packages for most of the people who brought us special gifts yesterday. Mother and I spent several hours driving around delivering them this afternoon.

July 5: Today the clothes chute [an opening on the 2nd floor for laundry to go down to the basement laundry room.] was full of dirty clothes again so I washed them all, 3 loads, and that is a lot of clothes to carry out in the yard, take down again and either put away or sprinkle for ironing.

July 8: Mother and Vernon left this morning about seven. .. Ten days is enough to have visitors around.

July 17: The Robinsons, bless them, are the most entertaining friends we have and Bette especially was in rare form at the dinner table.

July 19: Bette is such a nice girl to have around. She washes dishes and helps keep things neat as no-one in my own family will trouble doing.

August 9: It is a job to buy and carry home enough food for this family---not to mention preparing it.

Aug. 26: I feel so tired and nervous and the hot flashes are worse again. I wish I could go away somewhere all alone and just stay until I felt able to cope again.

EDITOR

In October, 1955, Gene and Dorothy took a two-week trip to Topeka, Kansas, where Grandma Allbert was keeping house for Vernon who had been divorced. They stopped in Peoria and Council Bluffs on the way.

DOROTHY (Diary)

Oct. 8: We reached Peoria---we drove 580 miles today, which is an awful lot. We are at Aunt Sadie's house where we always stay and Aunt Margie and Cousins Mildred and Sally were here to welcome us.

Oct. 9: Tonight there was a gathering of the clan for a supper here at Aunt Sadie's. All the women bring something and they are all such good cooks that the food is fit for a king.

Oct. 11: I always feel awkward at first when we come to Council Bluffs. Dad always seems delighted to have us but I never cared much for my stepmother, though she is nice when we visit here. She enjoys poor health and always has and her house is so dirty it makes me uncomfortable.

Oct. 12: Gene helped Dad put up most of the storm windows which pleased Dad very much. He doesn't look his 77 years at all but he shouldn't do such heavy work as the storm windows are.

Oct. 14: Mother seemed overjoyed to see us but we weren't here five minutes until she was crying and telling us how unhappy she is. . . . She is homesick for her old home and her old friends and neighbors.

Oct. 15: This vacation was supposed to give me a good rest and it is certainly doing that: Plenty of sleep and no excitement at all.

Oct. 22: The last day of our vacation trip and it has been one of the nicest ones. . . .We got to Gwen and Dixie Ellis

[Westinghouse and church friends] home in Beaver, Pa. about noon and we had such a nice visit with them. Sometimes it seems like there are no friends like old friends. {This was one of Dorothy's favorite quotations.} Home about 9:40. Our own home is more entertaining than any place else we go. John and Peggy say they are going to be married on Dec. 31 and Roger [Dayer] and Bobby on June 16th. Ruth and Roy [Rogers] are apparently making great progress too!

Nov. 14: Going out tires me more than anything.

Nov. 15: Sometimes I think it will be a relief when they are all married and gone but of course I will be terribly lonely then. But they <u>are</u> difficult sometimes or maybe it's me!

Nov. 23: I get so weary of constantly buying and preparing food but guess it is a pretty necessary occupation.

Dec. 21: Tonight the five of us had dinner together for what might be the last time all five of us will have a meal together alone.

EDITOR

      Since John Clarke was a Roman Catholic, and Peggy was a Baptist, they decided to have a small wedding in St. Andrew's Episcopal Church, just for family and close friends.

DOROTHY: (Diary)

December 31: This was our Peggy's Wedding Day. Everything seemed quite perfect. Even the weather co-operated by being much pleasanter than Dec. 31 usually is. It was fairly dry underfoot so we didn't need boots & the sun peeked out several times & there was no rain or snow. We were all dressed for the wedding in good time and Gene took several pictures.

Peggy looked perfectly beautiful!...The ceremony was beautiful. Afterward Gene & Mr. Clarke both took pictures & then we went on to the Park Lane [Restaurant] & a photographer was there to make the formal photos. Everyone at the Park Lane was wonderful to us. The dinner was delicious & we were all happy & gay. We came home afterward & the boys fixed the car with streamers & a "Just Married" sign, while Peggy changed her clothes and she threw her bouquet from the stairs. Kraussy [Ruth Krauss, Peggy's best friend] caught it and they were off on their honeymoon. They are driving to Syracuse tonight and on to New York tomorrow. After they left the others left one & two at a time....The Newly-weds called about 1:00 to wish us a Happy New Year. They sounded very happy & excited still and it was good to hear from them. And so, ended one of the most eventful days of our family's life: Our Peggy's Wedding Day. And so ended 1955.

EDITOR

1956 witnessed equally momentous changes in the Allbert family as Ruth graduated from Buffalo State

Teachers College and began teaching in California. (Ruth had finished college in three years.) Roberta married Roger after her junior year, but finished her degree at the University of Rochester, living in the dormitory during the week and returning home on the weekends. Roger started Medical School at the University of Buffalo. Roberta and Roger had a small apartment on Dorothy & Gene's 3rd floor. Meanwhile Peggy announced her pregnancy!

Gene and Dorothy continued with all their work and church responsibilities, adding more travel to their schedules, as they began visiting their out-of-town daughters. But Dorothy missed her daughters and was very lonely at times. A theme which recurs in her diary is her resentment of Gene's being out every night at some meeting and her ongoing effort to lose weight.

DOROTHY: (Diary)

<u>1956</u>

Feb. 21: I wish Gene liked to stay home & just plain relax & enjoy life a little better.

March 2: Gene hurt my feelings tonight. I had my fur coat on he put his arms around me and called me his "big brown bear".

March 3: [At Peg and John's home in Utica, NY.] Peg cooked a nice supper and tonight we went to the Show [movie]. I feel closer to Peg than I have since she was a little girl.

March 7: I am sure in a "Blue Funk" this week. I just don't want to work at all and I have all kinds of work that should be done. I did do a little house cleaning but not nearly as much as needs doing and as I could do if I'd settle down to it. I washed a couple of loads of clothes so at least I have the washing done now. I am so upset about the Westinghouse Strike. The union is just stalling around and if they reject the offer things will be right where they were almost five months ago.... Gene went to Prayer Meeting but when he came home he said "What a good night to stay in" and coming from him that really meant something.

March 10: Ruthie was home all day...I am so much more contented when someone is here with me.

March 11: We called on a couple who live near the church. Gene always wants to call on every one new he meets or else to entertain them in our home. I get so irked with him about it, because I don't think people expect to be called on any more or even care about it particularly.

March 13: I counted the church money tonight.

March 26: All our children will be home for Easter. I'm so glad!

April 3: Bobbie and I went to a Bakery this morning and ordered the biggest wedding cake they bake. We also ordered 5 lbs. of Petit Fours [fancy candies] and 10 lbs. of fancy cakes....Mrs. Dayer [Roger's mother] is going to make the Flower Girl's dress.

April 7: Enjoying lovely shower gifts.

April 8: Worked on the church books. Quarterly statements are due and are quite a job so that will keep me busy in any spare moments this week.

April 10: Another "running around" day but they are the ones I enjoy the most.

April 11: I've been able to lose 2 lbs. only in a month. It is *so* hard for me to diet when I have to cook so much and just naturally *love* to eat. Two pounds down is better than two lbs. up, and I am going to continue *trying*.

April 15: Ruthie planning to go to California to teach. I feel sick about the whole thing but I can see it is no use to try to oppose her.

April 19: I went down to the church and helped sort the things for the Rummage Sale tomorrow.... We worked hard for about three hours.

April 24: I love the days that I have the car because I can get around and do so many things and don't have to stay at home and feel lonely.

April 26: The housework is only about half as much as it used to be.

April 27: Cancer Crusade calls. [Dorothy went door to door for several charities.]

April 30: I am so discouraged about my weight. Addressing wedding invitations.

May 31: Roger is as thrilled with the wedding gifts as we are.

June 2: I feel so hurt and unappreciated at times, and the family think I am just pouty.

June 8: The gifts continue to arrive... Those kids are so well loved they don't know how lucky they are.

June 10: I'm afraid Ruthie feels her graduation is being eclipsed by Bobbie's wedding and I'm sorry.

June 11: Ruth's graduation was at 10:00 this morning at Kleinhan's [Music Hall] so we left home at 8:45 in order to get her there... Mother, Vernon & Aunt Sadie arrived just as we got home. It was quite a flurry to get lunch for everyone and get the visitors unpacked and settled. We are glad to see them and hope they will enjoy visiting us.

EDITOR

Roberta's wedding on June 16th was a large one which involved much planning and entertaining, both of local and of out-of-town guests. So, Dorothy, while happy, became exhausted.

DOROTHY: (Diary)

June 16: The Day of Days at last! And everything was quite perfect. The weather was cooler but no rain. This morning Gene & I had to pick up the Punch Bowls and get them to the church and there were people all over the house but we were all dressed---including the bride, by 1:00 so we had time to take pictures before we went. The ceremony was beautiful and only about ten minutes late starting. Both Ministers took part. [Roger was a Methodist and Roberta a Baptist] The receiving line was fun and all went smoothly at the reception. We were out on the lawn a lot and that made it nice. About fifty people came back to the house to see them leave but they didn't stay for supper. Thank Goodness!

EDITOR

Hardly had Roberta and Roger left for their honeymoon than Dorothy faced up to the question of Grandma Allbert's future. Vernon was about to be married (for the second time) and his new wife (Portia) refused to have Louise live with them. Dorothy had the unhappy task of telling her.

Another family crisis arose in July when Roy Rogers (Ruth's boyfriend) was awarded a Fulbright Fellowship to study in the Netherlands. This of course was a great honor for Roy. But Dorothy was upset because the reason Ruth was going to California to teach was because Roy had a job there! And now he was going to Europe!

DOROTHY (Diaries)

June 18: We told Grandma and I hope convinced her that if Vernon and Portia marry, she is to come and live with us. But that will be another problem.

July 16: Roy has decided to accept the Scholarship and Ruth is heartbroken. She feels she will lose him if they are separated so long and she has that darned contract to teach there because of him.

July 17: I am just furious with Roy about all of it.

July 22: Gene and I have both worked so hard for so many years that we hardly know what to do with ourselves except work. . . . Ruth played the piano for us. We are going to miss her so!

Aug. 1: I so hate being fat!

Dec. 10: Enjoying the peace and quiet of living alone.

Dec. 18: I took Agnes, my hairdresser, a Christmas gift. I bought her a nice flannelette house coat and hope she will like it. She is a widow with a young son to support and she is such a proud person she would never let on if things were tough for her but I'm sure they often are. She seemed pleased that I brought her a gift.

Dec. 21: Roberta got home for Christmas vacation this afternoon and Roger came for supper. We will have plenty of people here to eat for the next two weeks.

Dec. 22: I cleaned the spare bedroom and got it ready for Peg & John to use.

Dec. 24: This has been a terrible day! There was so much to do and I have just worked at top capacity all day long and as a result was too tired and cross this evening. I wanted everything so nice for Ruth's homecoming. Gene, Bobbie and Roger met her at the Air Port and I had dinner ready for them but then everyone was in a hurry . . .I was crabby to Ruth and made her feel bad.

1957

Jan. 1: I finally got started on a blanket for Peg's baby. It is real cute.

Jan. 2: Today I have really let down. The house is filthy but I'm ignoring it. . .the girls took the car and left so I was all alone at last and I laid down and just relaxed for a long time. We had Ruth's farewell dinner tonight and she requested Roast Lamb. We were all so relaxed and had such a nice time together and I thought why couldn't it have been this way all the time but there was just too much excitement.

Jan. 21: Today was Inauguration Day [for President Dwight D. Eisenhower]. I spent several hours just watching the TV. We surely live in an age of miracles.

EDITOR

One of the results of Ruth's move to California was renewed contact with Dorothy's mother. Dorothy had never told the children that her mother was alive. A half-sister, Evelyn Meeks, lived near Ruth, as did Dorothy's nephew, Eugene Glassey, Uncle Bert's son, whom Dorothy had taken care of when he was a baby in Raton. Ruthie contacted all of them after she moved to Mountain View, California. While Dorothy never explained her feelings for her mother, it seems clear that she resented the fact that her mother left her as a child and never took any responsibility for her thereafter. Furthermore, I suspect that Dorothy was ashamed of what she regarded as her mother's immoral behavior, since there seem to have been several men in her life.

DOROTHY: (Diary)

1957

Jan. 26: I wrote a long letter to my mother and my half-sister, Evelyn. It is good to be in touch with them again even though it has been so many years since I have seen them that I can hardly realize they are my relatives.

Feb. 1: To Utica to visit Peg and John. They greeted us with the news that John is changing jobs and they will be leaving Utica right away.

Feb. 13: I am so disgusted about my weight that I could jump out the window!

EDITOR

Because Peggy's baby was due in March, she and John decided that she should stay in Buffalo until after the baby was born, while he went to Denver to start a new job and find a place for them to live. Naturally Gene and Dorothy were happy to have her with them but it made for a full household!

DOROTHY: (Diary)

March 1: Gene and Peggy and John all arrived at almost the same time. Peg & John had the Station wagon loaded to the hilt and were pulling a big trailer equally loaded.

March 5: This is our Peggy's 24th birthday. It is so nice that we can have her with us. We have had the nicest time together these few days; she, her daddy and me.

March 9: Our granddaughter is here. She arrived about 1:00 this morning. ... We went to see Peggy and baby. We saw our little Mary Ellen and she is precious and Peggy is fine, too.

March 15: Roger and Bobbie got home tonight about suppertime so now there are six adults and one baby. [And one bathroom!]

March 26: John left for Denver today.... He hired a big Trailer and has all their things packed in it and the Station Wagon. Denver is a long way to haul all that.... Tonight Peggy was invited out to play bridge with some of her old High School friends and I kept the baby. She was really good too, and I am just crazy about her.

EDITOR

Despite the fact that she loved her new grandchild, Dorothy was a little overwhelmed having Peggy and the baby living there, as well as Roger and Bobbie, which required much more hauling of groceries and extra cooking, plus more cleaning. Naturally Dorothy wanted to show off Mary Ellen to all of her friends, so that led to entertaining many visitors! And her church work continued as usual.

DOROTHY: (Diary)

March 27: For some strange reason I am just so used up I am good for nothing. It is always such a relief when I have the Missionary meeting over and I had great plans of all the housework I was going to do but I was just <u>too</u> tired.

April 1: April Fool's Day but there was no fooling about the work I <u>had</u> to get done as the Gleaners Class meeting was here.... All went well though, as far as I know.

April 2: I am just tired of everything and everybody, I'm afraid.

April 5: I sure am in a slump. I enjoy having Peggy and the baby here so much and I just love to spend all my time with them so I have gotten so far behind with my housework it has me all upset. Gene is working so terribly hard and not getting enough rest and he seems to feel I'm neglecting him so he is irritable. And I am sick unto death of buying food and cooking meals and of my responsibilities as Missionary Society President.

April 11: Tonight I spent the whole evening working on the church offering. That is a job that must be done every week and it takes quite a while to do it too.

EDITOR

Dorothy accompanied Peggy and Mary Ellen on their trip to Denver by train. Afterwards Dorothy continued on to Council Bluffs, Iowa, to see her father and step mother, and then to Topeka, Kansas, to see Grandma Allbert and Vernon.

DOROTHY: (Diary)

April 18: We had to change trains in Chicago. I'm so glad I am with Peggy as it is such bustle and confusion and there was so much to carry and it seemed so hard to get a porter. We had two berths on the train and they put a hammock for baby over Peggy's bed. She was fussy for hours but settled down again when Peggy got her into bed.

April 24: Tonight Vernon's fiancé, Portia Anderson, came in and we went through a lot of the things to see what we wanted. Portia took a lot of things for her sorority rummage sale.

April 25: I feel sorry for Mother. She has just really become adjusted to living in Topeka and now she has to be uprooted again. It is really tough to get old.

April 27: We have a Sleeper [train] to Chicago.

April 30. I am really glad Mother is here [in Buffalo] or I'd be terribly lonesome.

May 2: Tonight Gene wanted me to go with him to a Conference on Evangelism. I went though I didn't really want to.

May 7: Gene came home feeling about as low as he ever gets. They are pushing them terribly out at work.

May 12: This is the first Mother's Day Gene's mother has been with him since he was 18 years old and it is the first I've ever had without two of my children. I can't help feeling sad about Peggy and Ruth being so far away but I am so glad Bobbie is still here.

May 14: Gene had invited a young Italian engineer who is working with him for dinner tonight. I _do_ wish Gene didn't take entertaining so seriously. I am always _so_ ill-at-ease and uncomfortable with people I don't know. However, I try not to show it and this young man was really very nice---he was the very essence of politeness. Europeans have so much nicer manners than we Americans do.

May 24: Gene went back to work [after dinner] and Mother and I played a few games of Chinese checkers.

June 1: Gene went fishing most of the day.

June 2: Bobbie arrived and is unpacking. It appears someone is forever either moving in or moving out here.

June 8: Tonight we all listened to Billy Graham on TV. He is a great evangelist and doing a great work but he doesn't say a thing I haven't heard many times.

June 9: Roberta's graduation from the U[niversity] of R[ochester]. Thomas E. Dewey was the speaker... We are enormously proud of her.

June 13: Mother watches me so closely all the time that it makes me very nervous.

June 15: Gene left at 5:00 a.m. to go fishing and then the men were going to work at Camp Vick [a new Baptist camp which was being developed nearby].

June 27: Gene is like a little boy the way he is anticipating his fishing trip with Ralph Immel [a Westinghouse associate].

July 2: Another interesting day! Maybe I'm a little conceited but I don't think many people have as interesting a life as I have.

EDITOR

In July, 1957, Dorothy visited her mother whom she had not seen in 33 years. She traveled to California by train to visit Ruth but she also saw her mother and half-sister, Evelyn Meeks. Gradually Dorothy's natural sympathy overcame her long-held resentment of her mother's abandoning her as a child. By July 16, she writes: "I feel more drawn to her each time we are together". After returning home she began sending clothes and gifts to her mother.

Dorothy enjoyed her visit to Ruthie's home in Mountain View, California, where Ruth and two friends from Buffalo had rented a house. Dorothy also visited her cousin, Eugene Glassey, whom she had not seen since he was a baby in New Mexico. Now he was a father with children of his own.

From San Francisco, Dorothy flew to Denver to be with Peggy and John and Mary Ellen. At last Dorothy was beginning to reap the benefits of all those hard years of work and sacrifice!

DOROTHY: (Diary)

July 4: I am taking the Santa Fe Chief and it is made up in Chicago. It is a very fine train with a Vista Dome car from which you can get a fine view of the scenery.

July 6: I went up in the Vista Dome and watched the sun rise over the desert. It was beautiful and we also saw some beautiful mountain scenery from there to Bakersfield. I got to San Francisco at 1:30 and was really ready to get off. My half-sister, Evelyn Meeks, her husband George, and Ruthie all met me and took me right to Evelyn's.

July 7: The first thing this morning I was informed that my mother (and Evelyn's) was flying from Ft. Worth, Texas and would get here tonight.

I was kind of upset as I haven't seen my mother for 33 years and she is a stranger to me, really, but there was nothing I could do about it.... my mother arrived about midnight. My emotions are too mixed to describe.

July 8: It seems so strange after 33 years to be with my mother again. She is only 66 but the years have not been kind to her & she has had a hard life. She is frail & partially crippled. Today was Evelyn's birthday and Ruth had invited us all out to Mountain View for dinner tonight.

July 11: Ruth fixed broiled steaks for supper and afterward we went over to my cousin Eugene Glassey's. He has a lovely young wife and two beautiful children, a boy 5 and a baby girl 6 months. They have a beautiful home, too.

July 13: This has been a beautiful and very interesting day. Mother and Evelyn came out and we left about nine o'clock to drive to Carmel by-the-Sea, which is one of the beauty spots of this area. The drive was beautiful and we stopped in Monterey where the 17 Mile Drive begins and were all hungry so we had a picnic lunch .... The Cypress trees, the huge rocks and the gift shops and wonderful Beach at Carmel were all so interesting.

July 14: Met the Grimes [Turtle Creek friends] who took me to a nice Cafeteria for dinner and then we went to the

Cliff House and to Muir Woods and saw some of the beautiful big redwood trees.

July 16: The plane trip from San Francisco to Denver was very interesting. We flew over Yosemite and saw "Half Dome" over Utah and Nevada and finally right over the summit of the Rockies. Oh how cruel and jagged they looked...Peggy and Mary Ellen met me and I was <u>so</u> glad to see them. The baby is just a little darling.

July 19: Peggy & John took me out to the most wonderful place to eat that I was ever in. It is an ultramodern building with a regular outside setting indoors. We went in the Cocktail Lounge first & I had a glass of mild wine & then we had a wonderful fish dinner complete with organ music.

July 20: The plane trip was a wonderful experience... it is good to be home again.

July 22: We use the [clothes] dryer for the first time and I'm quite pleased with it and surprisingly enough, so is Mother.

Aug. 18: Ruth and Roy are engaged and she is so happy. As soon as he got to California they left to visit with his family in Medford, Oregon and as soon as they got there he gave her the diamond ring which he bought last summer. They are planning to be married in California at Thanksgiving so we will have another nice trip.

Sept. 6: Mother is just so happy and contented now that she is going back to Raton for a while. She is like a different person and we are getting along fine.

Sept. 8: Gene was elected Vice-President of the N[ew] Y[ork State] Baptist Men's group. More work!

November 22: Ruth and Roy were at the San Francisco Airport to meet us and took us in to George & Evelyn's where we had a nice lunch. It is good to see them again.

Nov. 23: After supper we came out to Mountain View with Ruth & Roy. Their house is very nice.

EDITOR

The final big event of 1957 was Ruth and Roy's wedding in California. Bobbie was teaching school and Roger was in his second year of Medical School. They decided they could not afford for Bobbie to fly to California for the wedding. Later, this decision was much regretted, but at that time, it seemed necessary. And so sister Peggy served as Ruth's only attendant. Grandma Allbert had been visiting the Clarkes in Denver so she traveled to California with Peggy for the wedding and Gene and Dorothy flew out from Buffalo.

DOROTHY: (Diary)

Nov. 25: We visited Ruth's school room this afternoon and listened to her Fourth Graders read. She is a fine teacher and her youngsters are sweet.

Nov. 28: Well this was the Wedding Day as well as Thanksgiving. . . Peggy wore red velvet and Ruth wore Peggy's wedding dress and veil and they both looked just beautiful. The wedding was in a small chapel and there were just 21 of us present. Roland Rogers, Roy's cousin and best man, had just recovered from flu and he passed out during the ceremony but the minister went right on. . . . We liked Roy's people.

EDITOR

After the wedding Dorothy and Gene flew to Denver to visit Peggy's family and learned that Peggy was expecting her second child. They had a wonderful visit with Peggy, John and Mary Ellen for a week, returning to Buffalo on December 7.

DOROTHY: (Diary)

Dec. 8: Everyone seemed so glad to have us back it was heartwarming.

Dec. 11: I have to admit that I really have an awfully pleasant life!

Dec. 22: This afternoon Gene & I decorated our Christmas tree. The girls always did the Christmas tree since they were little but no girls were here to do it.

EDITOR

On this poignant note, another chapter of Gene and Dorothy's life---one focused on raising three daughters, came to a conclusion.

CHAPTER IV:

GENE AND DOROTHY, 1958-1973:

Life Begins at 48!

EDITOR

Now that their daughters were raised and married, Gene and Dorothy began a new phase of their marriage, characterized by less work and more fun. By 1964 their daughters had produced ten grandchildren! Since Ruth lived in California and Peggy in Denver, Dorothy and Gene made many trips West, to see the new arrivals. In addition, Ruth and Peggy brought their families home to Buffalo at least once a year. Thus, the Allbert family was able to remain close, despite the distances separating them.

Because Roberta and Roger stayed in Buffalo, except for two years in the military, Gene and Dorothy were able to help them with their children and in many other ways as well. After finishing Medical School in 1960, Roger embarked on a one-year internship, which was followed by a five-year residency in surgery. Roberta taught school some of the time but she also went to graduate school, first for a Master's degree, and later for a Ph. D., both in history. They could not have done this without the help of Roberta's parents.

Happily, Gene and Dorothy's social life expanded just as Gene's work responsibilities decreased. By the late '60s, the young engineers at Westinghouse whom he had trained, began to assume management positions.

Since Gene had never received a college degree, he was shifted back to the drafting department, where he now was working for engineers who formerly worked for him! But happily, the Allberts' life began to be filled with leisure activities which they loved, such as bowling, playing cards and fishing. Dorothy joined the Westinghouse Women's Club and the Suburban Women's Club where she formed many new friends.

After the calm and prosperity of the Eisenhower years in the 1950s, long submerged social issues, involving racism, colonialism and women's rights, emerged in the 1960s to create political crises and rapid social change in American life. President John F. Kennedy had been elected in 1960 in a very close contest against the Republican candidate, Richard Nixon. Hardly had Kennedy assumed office when he faced the Cuban Missile Crisis, which involved the threat of nuclear war with the Soviet Union. Happily, that crisis was settled peacefully. But in addition, the U. S. was becoming deeper involved in the Vietnam War.

In addition, President Kennedy and his successor, Vice President Lyndon B. Johnson, faced an increasingly explosive civil rights movement. Led by the articulate Baptist Minister, Rev. Martin Luther King, the Civil Rights Movement succeeded in convincing President Lyndon B. Johnson in 1964, to force though Congress the first Civil Rights Law since the Civil War. During the 1950s, France had attempted to reassert control of its former colony, French Indo-China. In response, the Vietnamese people, who had declared their independence in 1945, fought the return of the French. American postwar policy had been to support an independent South Vietnam and to characterize the Northern Vietnamese nationalists as Communists under the control of Moscow and Peking. After the French withdrew from Indochina and the forces of Ho Chi Minh expanded their control, American involvement grew steadily.

Opposition to the Vietnam War grew rapidly, especially after the draft was imposed. At the same time, the feminist movement, led by Gloria Steinem, began making demands for equality for women. All three movements proved very unsettling to adult Americans, as they watched their children demonstrating against the government and refusing to serve in the military.

While Dorothy and Gene were not directly involved in any of these movements, their daughter, Roberta, was an active supporter and participant in all three. Like most of their contemporaries of the World War II generation, the Allberts were shocked that young people and leaders of the clergy could question the legitimacy of the Vietnam War, and refuse to serve when drafted. Nor did Dorothy understand why Roberta wanted to have a career. However, as Baptists, Gene and Dorothy sympathized with Dr. Martin Luther King and the Civil Rights struggle.

Even more disturbing in the 1960s was the assassination of three American leaders: First, President Kennedy in 1963, then Martin Luther King in 1967 and finally, Attorney General Robert Kennedy (the late

President's brother) in 1968. Little wonder that many Americans felt that their country was coming apart!

While Gene and Dorothy were concerned about all of these crises, (especially Roberta's involvement) they focused on two more personal worries: One was selling their home and moving to the suburbs; the other was the decision to leave Delavan Ave. Baptist Church. Other immediate concerns were the care of Gene's mother and Dorothy's health. She developed a condition known as interstitial cystitis which caused intense abdominal pain and which limited her activities much of the time. Unfortunately, there was no known cure.

In hopes of improved clarity, I have created sub-topics for this chapter rather than proceeding chronologically.

Grandchildren and Travel

DOROTHY (Diary)

<u>1959</u>

May 17: The nicest thing has happened. Lois McNerney---one of the girls' old high school crowd---is driving to California for Sharon Koch's [Ruth's former roommate] wedding June 6th. Lois's husband can't miss work to go and she wanted company so I'm going! I'm just so excited I can't keep still. I'll come back on the train as Lois has other plans about the return trip and I'll stop in Denver, so I'll see both my girls within the next month!

June 3: [Ruth's home in Mountain View, California] We sure had a long day yesterday and I'm pretty tired from the trip but today has been very busy again. Sharon came over this morning and she and Lois went to San Francisco and I had the use of Sharon's car. Edna Culp is here, taking care of my cousin's children and my dear old Uncle Bert who was like a father to me until I was fifteen years old and whom I hadn't seen since, is here too and I drove over and got him and we went over to see Edna together and had a good visit together.

June 7: We had planned a picnic up in the mountains at Portola State Park. Evelyn, George, Mother and Uncle Bert were to meet us at the park.

June 11: George and Evelyn met my train in San Francisco. Mother seemed overjoyed to see me but I just can't really respond to her affection though I try to be nice.

June 13: ...on the California Zepher---an ultra-modern train that goes clear through to Chicago. I am taking the train instead of flying to Denver as the route is famous for its beautiful scenery. The train goes through the Feather River Valley up through the Sierra Nevada mountains. Several people have seemed interested in talking to me today. I flatter myself that this indicates that I look like an interesting person but perhaps I only look harmless.

June 15: [Denver] Between the bright Colorado sun and the wide-awake babies it was very easy to get up early. Mary Ellen made up with me in just a little while and Johnnie was friendly right away. He is just an adorable baby---one of those fat, rosy blond and good-natured babies that is irresistible, and Mary Ellen has always been extra-special of course.

June 20: Peggy and I have just had such a nice time together taking care of these two darling babies. I hate to leave them but will be seeing them again in six weeks.

June 23: [Buffalo} It is so nice to just have Gene and myself to cook for. The meals are just no task at all and getting meals has been such a big job [for] so long.

EDITOR

When Roberta became pregnant in 1959, she and Roger moved to the Buffalo Housing Projects. The 3rd Allbert grandchild, Lawrence Eugene Dayer, was born on June 28, 1959 at Children's Hospital. In late July, Gene and Dorothy traveled by car to Yellowstone National Park and afterwards to Denver. On their way home, they picked up Grandma Allbert and drove her back to Buffalo.

DOROTHY: (Diary)

<u>1959</u>

29 June: We went to the hospital again tonight and took Elva [Roger's mother] with us and we agree that our grandson is wonderful and Bobbie is fine now. This was our 29th anniversary.

31 July: [Denver] Today is little John's first birthday so we were able to be at his birthday party. Mother Allbert has been here since Tuesday but is leaving for Peoria tomorrow. She looks just wonderful and has been very pleasant to me this evening. Peggy always seems so glad to see us.

August 1: Gene and John got up about 2:00 a.m. to go up in the mountains fishing with some men from John's office so they haven't been around to bother us at all today.

August 10: We got to my friend's home in North Platte, Nebraska about 2:30. Lois Kallin Hogel and I were friends in Council Bluffs 30 years ago and though we've not seen each other since 1940 we've kept in touch and it was so good to see her again.

August 11: Our next destination was the home of my stepsister in Council Bluffs, Iowa. We got here just before noon and she has air-conditioning, which made it wonderful. We talked quite a lot about the problem of my Dad. She said she didn't know why he left there and went down south, as both she and Wallace [her husband] wanted him to stay.

August 12: Every time I'm in Council Bluffs I hope I won't have to come back. There are unhappy associations here from years ago and I just never really feel like one of them. It was a long, hot drive to Peoria and we got here about six o'clock. Aunt Sadies's home is nice and she always makes us feel so welcome. Mother A. seems happy to see us too and she is looking forward so much to getting back to Buffalo. Wish I could say the same.

August 14: Peoria to Buffalo---700 miles. This was my 49th birthday but it hardly seems worth mentioning.

August 18: Ruth Rogers arrived.

August 26: After supper we hurried out to the Air Port to meet Peggy and her babies. They came here after two weeks at Cape Cod with the Clarke grandparents. We are so glad to see them again!

August 27: Tonight we had the happy experience of having all three of our girls together for dinner so it was very special.

Dec. 9: After bowling I stopped by to see Bobbie and Larry and had a nice visit with them. I don't know how I could go on living if they weren't here.

EDITOR

The frequent travels continued in 1960 as more grandchildren arrived. First Dorothy flew to Denver in June for the birth of Peggy's 3rd child (Mark); then in November she and Gene flew to Denver and California where they met Phyllis Jean Rogers, Ruth's first baby.

DOROTHY: (Diary)

1960

June 29: I was in Denver by noon and Peggy and her babies were at the Air Port to meet me.

July 5: Well today was the day! We have another grandson- - - Mark Franklin.

July 9: John went to the hospital for Peggy and they were all home again by 3:30. Little Mary E. was just so happy to see her Momma again and she is just in ecstasy over the "tiny baby".

July 17: John and Mary Ellen drove me to the airport this morning. She is such a nice little girl and very interested in airplanes. Gene met me and of course we stopped to see Bobbie and Larry and tonight we went to see "Carousel" at Melody Fair [a summer theater]. Enjoyed it a lot.

September 18: At last we have another granddaughter [Phyllis Jean Rogers}. We are so happy to get another little girl. Ruth talked to us herself and her voice just vibrated with happiness. I am so thankful they are both all right. She got along fine.

Nov. 20: [Denver} It is so wonderful to see Peg and John and their babies again. Peggy always seems so happy to have us and little Mary Ellen remembers me and is so glad to see me. Johnny is as cute as ever but not very friendly yet and little Mark is an adorable baby but just now he has a very bad cold.

Nov. 25: [San Francisco} Roy was at the Airport to meet us and we met lovely little Phyllis Jean as soon as we got home. She is a perfectly beautiful little baby and so sweet and good.

Nov. 28: Roy took us to Evelyn's. Mother and Evelyn were overjoyed as they always seem to be when I come and Mother was so interested in meeting Gene. I never really enjoy being here but they seem to like having me so much I try to act as though I reciprocate.

Nov. 29: Tonight we were invited over to my cousin Gene Glassey's for dessert. Uncle Bert was there and it was sure nice to see the dear old fellow again. Later, Gene showed us through his machine shop.

EDITOR

In spring, 1961, Gene and Dorothy took a trip South and visited her father in Virginia. That summer, both Ruth and Peggy's families came to Buffalo again.

DOROTHY: (Diary)

1961

April 25: Independence, VA. Saw Dad today. He lives with an elderly couple, typical mountaineers. They are kind and good people.

Aug. 2: Peggy, John and 3 children got here about 4. We're so glad to see them and the children are sweet.

Aug. 10: The Clarkes left this morning. I'm just exhausted but it was still hard to say goodbye.

1962

Feb. 15: Roger called at 9:30 and to our surprise and delight we have a baby girl!

Tonight, after dinner was over and Larry ready for bed [Two-year-old Larry was staying with Nana and Boppa] I took "Moma Dayer" and we went in to see our new granddaughter. She is a beautiful baby and Bobbie is fine too. Her name is Cynthia Louise.

EDITOR

The Allberts' travels continued in 1962, with a trip South in May by Dorothy and a friend, to West Virginia to visit Dorothy's father and then a summer trip West by Gene and Dorothy to the Seattle World's Fair, followed by visits to Ruth in California and Peggy in Denver.

DOROTHY: (Diary)

1962

May 4: In West Virginia with Leila Burns [a Delavan Ave. church friend]. Leila is the only person I know who enjoys playing cards as much as I do.

May 5: After breakfast I went to my cousin's, Can and Carrie Edwards. They are real Hill Billies and live way back in the mountains but they are wonderful people and seemed so glad to see me. After we had lunch they went with me about 20 miles to another cousin's farm near Sparta, North Carolina and they too gave me a royal welcome. My father lives with them. He doesn't seem especially glad to see me.

June 30: Began trip to Seattle, Washington, World's Fair.

July 13: [California] We reached Ruth's home about seven o'clock. Ruth looks well and her pregnancy isn't very evident as yet . . . .. Phyllis is just a living doll.

July 20 [Denver]: John and Peggy have a beautiful new home and they always make us feel so welcome and the children are all just as sweet as they can be. Little Kathleen doesn't seem as rosy and robust as the others have been.

July 27: To Peoria. Mother Allbert has been very ill and has failed a lot this year.

EDITOR

Mother Allbert returned to Buffalo with Gene and Dorothy, where she lived until November, when she and Dorothy flew to Chicago. Dorothy transferred Louise to a plane for Peoria, while she continued to Denver.

DOROTHY: (Diary)

Nov. 22: [Denver] Thanksgiving Day. I think this is the first time in our 32 years that Gene and I have spent Thanksgiving Day apart. [Gene celebrated Thanksgiving with Bobbie's family].

Nov. 25: Roy called to say that we have a new grandson, David Allbert Rogers.

Nov. 27: [California] Little Phyllis is making up with me very happily and she is just a little doll---a wonderful child.

Nov. 28: Tonight was a typical first night. Ruth coped with Davey, Roy with P.J. and I with dinner and the dishwasher and at last peace prevailed.

Dec. 7: Uncle Bert and I took the 10:06 Commuters train to San Francisco today. My cousin Gene took us to the train. Evelyn met us and took us to her home for a pleasant lunch with her and mother.

Dec. 14: It was hard to say Good-by to Ruth and darling Phyllis but I try to make farewells as painless as possible.

EDITOR

Dorothy's diary for 1963 is very sketchy, with little detail. She was experiencing some major health problems caused by the cystitis. However, in October they rented a trailer and traveled South, to visit Dorothy's cousins and then continued to Florida. They traveled as far as the Florida Keys! Dorothy kept a full record of that trip including mileage and every penny spent. They were gone almost a month and drove over 15,000 miles. The trip to Florida was a trial run, to see how they liked living in Florida where many of their friends had retired.

DOROTHY: (Diary)

1963

October 24: Went back in the mountains this morning to see Can and Carrie Edwards. . . . They are such simple yet generous people they just want to share all they have which isn't much.

Oct. 26: We drove and drove and finally reached Orlando and found a trailer park about 3:30.

Oct. 27: Silver Springs, FL: We took a trip in a glass-bottomed boat and another boat trip up the Silver river and visited the Aquatorium and the Prince of Peace Memorial and had a nice dinner in the restaurant. The Florida weather is all that is claimed for it.

Oct. 31: The drive along the Everglades was most interesting---we saw so many birds, cranes, ducks and snake birds. . . we started our journey out the Florida Keys. We stopped and had a cooked meal in Key Largo.

The trip out here was just beautiful with the Atlantic Ocean on the left and the Gulf on the right, both sparkling in the sunshine and in full view of the highway most of the time. We found a Trailer Park near Key West, left the Trailer and drove on to the beach and Gene fished and I walked on the sand and waded in the ocean water... It appears each day of this vacation is full of pleasant experiences.

Nov. 1: Finally we reached the Hollywood Beach Trailer Park and this one is the Utopia of Trailer Parks. They use a jeep to park the trailer for us, the Bath House is large and tiled and sparkling clean and the Ocean and beautiful Beach are only a few yards away. It costs $3.50 a night but is worth it. We took a walk on the Beach and got our feet wet... Gene fished a while and then we took a ride around Hollywood. It is just fabulously beautiful.

Nov. 2: We are both so delighted with this place we decided to stay over here today and just enjoy the beach and the ocean and have a rest from visiting, sight-seeing and driving.

Gene was up early and had a dip before breakfast. I went in the water, too, later, and it is just wonderful. He fished and I took a long "constitutional" up the beach, wading most of the time.

After we showered, lunched and rested, we cleaned up and went to visit an old and dear friend from Turtle Creek days, Gladys Stewart Ross. She was married only about 1½ years ago and they have a beautiful home but her husband is very ill. It seems too bad when she found her love so late and now it looks like she won't have him long. Now Gene is out fishing again in the moonlight. The moon has been full and these warm nights with a full moon are all the songwriters claim. When he comes in we'll have some coffee and a piece of apple pie which Gladys had baked for us.

Nov. 4: W went sightseeing in St. Augustine, first to the Lightner Museum and it has more of the interesting and beautiful things than any museum I was ever in.

Nov. 8: Arrived home after driving 15,589 miles!

Nov. 22: Horror! President Kennedy was assassinated in Texas.

Nov. 25: Funeral on TV: Most inspiring but <u>so</u> sad.

EDITOR

The youthful President Kennedy, who had succeeded President Eisenhower in 1961 had captured the imagination and admiration of Americans who were fascinated by the glamour of his young wife, Jackie and the appeal of their two young children.

American optimism faded after Kennedy's death when Vice-President Johnson became President and the expansion of American involvement in the Vietnam war necessitated the first peacetime draft.

Dorothy does not seem to have kept a diary in 1964. If she did, it has been lost. However, it is certain that Stephanie Clarke was born in September in Denver, and Roger Edward Dayer was born in Buffalo on November 26th. Dorothy was in Denver when young

Roger was born. She and Eugene continued to travel a great deal in 1965. They particularly enjoyed their trip to the Maritime Provinces in Canada that summer, so much so that Eugene wrote a full account. Much later he also described his love of fishing.

GENE: (Essay, 1990s)

I have a passion for fishing. This passion did not exist until I had the right equipment and used it successfully. The strong desire to go fishing developed when my son-in-law, John Clarke, gave me a fishing pole with an open-face spinning reel with the line wound on it, ready to use. Then, on our first trip to his home in Utica, New York, he took a friend and me fishing in the Adirondack Park. We each caught a trout, and then cooked them on a fire built on the riverbank. This was part of our breakfast. It was the start of my passion.

The desire to fish has had a part in all of my travels ever since this experience.... There were two places to fish near my home in Buffalo, New York: the Niagara River and the pond at our church camp [Camp Vick]. The river did not produce fish easily, but the pond was productive. A trip on a small party-boat out of Halifax, Nova Scotia, was a joy for me. I asked the skipper if I could go up on the bow of the boat and he said yes. He would bait my hook, and I lowered it into the ocean. As soon as the bait reached the 40-foot depth, a fish would take the lure. I reeled it in, the skipper took it off the line and baited the hook and I repeated the action. I caught fish until we left the area for port.

This passion has caused me to fish in the Atlantic Ocean at Halifax and Florida, all along the Gulf coast, the Pacific Ocean, two of the Great Lakes and many places in between.

NEW HOUSE

GENE: (Autobiography)

My wife, Dorothy, thought we should look for a smaller house. She started to do this early in 1960. Dorothy found several houses to look at and I was not impressed with any until she showed me the one on 82 South Drive, Eggertsville. This was the house we should buy and we did. We moved into it in September, 1960. 426 La Salle sold for $14,900 and 82 South Drive cost $23,750. I was always pleased with this house and we lived there until November 1987, when we moved to California. We sold the house for $76, 500 in September 1987. The house had seven rooms, two baths and a full basement. I made the studio room the one with the 80 by 80-inch window, into my activity room for all my camera equipment. I installed the church door workbench with the machinist vise in the back of the basement. The former owners had left all of the house clean, so when we moved our furniture in we were ready to live there.

DOROTHY: (Diary)

<u>1960</u>

Aug. 1: We have decided to get at the business of finding ourselves another house if we are going to, and made a date to look at one tomorrow. I am so excited from

seeing nice houses I can hardly sleep at night. I was awake half the night thinking about that lovely little house and wondering if my furniture would fit in and so today I went out and measured the spaces I was in doubt about. We liked the place more than ever. We went over tonight and offered the lady $22,500. She wanted $25,000 but she is anxious to sell so we agreed at last on $23,750. We are thrilled but scared. This morning the first thing I got ready and went down [Bailey Avenue] and talked to Mr. Meyer who is the manager of the bank where we do most of our business. He was very helpful and said we could be reasonably confident they will loan us the necessary funds to buy this new house.

Aug. 10: Went to the bank and the lawyer's office again today and Mr. Meyer had an even better offer ready. He is going to loan us $10,000 on the house we own until we can sell it and put a $12,500 mortgage on the new house. Our lawyer read the contract and brought it here to be signed and tonight we went over to the new place and gave Mrs. Prochazka $1000 and she signed the contract. So now we have $1200 paid on our Dream House.

Aug. 14: My 50th birthday. Am going to start the count down now. If I counted back, I could be 20 years younger in 10 years! I do hate to be 50 but I don't feel old. My life is so much pleasanter than when I was 20 or 30 that it takes some of the pain out of being 50. My husband took me to dinner at Laube's [Old Spain Restaurant] and they played Happy Birthday to me and brought a big piece of cake with candles on it. Tonight, Bobbie had us down there. I don't know what we'd do without her!

Aug. 18: It makes me feel sad to think about selling this home we have loved so well and been so happy in, but that is life.

Sept. 13: This has been a Red Letter Day! Some people came to look at the house and they loved it and signed the contract and put $500 down on it tonight. We can hardly believe it!

Oct. 23: Gene worked all afternoon putting up pictures, etc. and stowing away his possessions in the drawers in the studio room. He is to have that room for his things and he is so pleased.

Dec. 26: Gene spent most of the day working in the basement. He built some nice shelves down there and is enjoying getting his workbench and tools put away. I hope he will be interested in keeping this basement clean and nice.

LIVING WITH LOUISE ALLBERT

EDITOR

Between 1959 and 1965, Grandma Allbert spent most of her time with Gene and Dorothy. However, when they traveled, she went to stay with her sister, Sadie, in Peoria. These were difficult years, both for Louise and Dorothy.

DOROTHY: (Diary)

<u>1959</u>

Jan. 8: Mother gets much disgruntled because I won't let her do all the washing and ironing but she really isn't able and anyway I'm not a parasite.

Feb. 2: I'm beginning to hate to see Monday come. This morning Mother was in the cellar when I came down and I went down and asked her if she was doing my washing and she just began to cry and tremble and was upset all day. I told her not to be so upset that I only want her to be happy and contented but she can't seem to believe that I do. I certainly don't know what to do to make her happier except to turn all the housework over to her and she isn't able to do it anyway.

Feb. 4: When I got home Mother was waiting for me to read a letter she had received from Vernon and it was really something. Apparently, Mother wrote him that she'd like to rent a place and live in Topeka for a while but he said if she did it would cause trouble between him and Portia. Portia is a really queer person. She doesn't want to "share her life" with Mother---or anyone else scarcely---even to the extent of eating a meal together. I just don't see how anyone could be so selfish and cruel and I'm amazed that Vernon would write such a letter to his mother. She is heartbroken and I'd like to scalp him and his Portia!

Feb. 5: Mother seems to have decided now that we aren't so bad to her after all and she is going to wait until late in the Spring to go out West. She wants Aunt Margie to come here for a visit and then she'll go back with her. So, we wrote Margie and invited her. Poor Mother is being very brave but that was such a cruel letter Vernon wrote her. No mother who has brought up a family deserves to be treated like that. Kenneth and Beth [Eugene's brother and his wife] have acted that way right along but I sure never expected Vernon to though I'm sure it is Portia's fault. I told him she was a queer and to look around some more but he wouldn't listen, and now he's stuck with her. Maybe she'll decide not to "share her life with him" someday too! [And she did!]

Feb. 10: Mother was thru ironing today before I had my breakfast and then she had nothing to do the rest of the day. She won't read anything in the way of fiction, just the Bible and articles about serious and weighty matters.

1960

Jan. 2: Grandma Allbert has lived with us for 19 months.

Jan. 4: Tonight it just seemed as though something impelled me to go up and talk to mother and I was so glad I did for she was crying and feeling so badly. She says she just doesn't feel as though she is wanted anywhere. I tried to be comforting.

Jan. 10: I try to go in Mother's room and watch TV with her a little so she won't feel so lonely.

Jan. 14: Mother has more vim and vitality than 10 average women and I'm afraid she'll live to be 100.

March 26: My day of Deliverance again! We put Mother on the train at 8:00 this morning. She says she is never coming back. I feel badly that our living together hasn't worked out better but I guess two women in one house just never works. I've tried to be nice---I've wanted her to be happy---but she just makes me so tense I can hardly live.

EDITOR

In February 1961, Dorothy noted that Grandma Allbert wanted to come back to Buffalo, but she responded: "Not before May". Gene and Dorothy were going to West Virginia to visit her father. Louise was with the Allberts again from May until July, 1961; then not again until August 1962. Gene and Dorothy had several trips planned and were busy with their new granddaughter, Cindy Lou Dayer. In July, they drove to the World's Fair in Seattle and then to Ruth's in California.

DOROTHY: (Diary)

1962

July27: Mother Allbert has been very ill and has failed a lot this year.

Sept. 8: Mother has been so pleasant and seems to feel so good and to be so happy. I just don't mind having her with us this time because she is so agreeable. We watched the Miss America contest tonight. It was very interesting

Sept. 20: I worried all night about Mother [after gall bladder surgery]. I went into the hospital and found her awake and in about the sweetest humor I've ever seen her. It was such a relief! I stayed with her until she had her dinner and helped her eat.

Nov. 20: To me it is always exciting to be leaving on an airplane. Our flight left Buffalo promptly at 8:00 and we were in Chicago in less than two hours. I had ordered a wheelchair for Mother and I expected her to be balky about it but she said it was a real help. We had a wait of more than an hour and then I put her on the plane for Peoria so she is off my back for a little while at least.

1963

Feb. 28: Had a pathetic letter from Mother. I feel so badly about shutting her out but we just can't live together.

1965

June 2: My cousin wants Mother to come back East. I don't want her but how can I refuse?

June 19: Mother arrived by plane at 2:00. She is so frail and feeble and rested a long time after she got here.

July 18: I took Mother to the plane.

Oct. 19: I was wakened by the phone at 9:15 with the news that Mother A. died suddenly this morning. Aunt Sadie found her on the kitchen floor.

EDITOR

In route to Raton for the funeral, the Allberts flew to Denver where Kenneth (Eugene' brother) met them and then they drove to Raton together.

DOROTHY: (Diary)

Oct. 22: Aunt Sadie is here [in Raton] and Vernon and Aunt Margie arrived after we did.

Oct. 23: We had Mother's funeral today. It was in the Baptist church where she and Dad both belonged and now she is at rest.

DECISION TO LEAVE DELAVAN CHURCH

EDITOR

In recent years Dorothy and Gene had become more and more dissatisfied with the Delavan Avenue Church, as Dorothy's diary makes clear.

DOROTHY: (Diary)

<u>1962</u>

May 22: Missionary Society: We had a very nice meeting and luncheon with installation of officers---I'm to be White Cross Chairman next year---we practiced a dumb old play which we are to give at the House Party next month. Gene and I do at least three times as much work and give at least twice as much money as anyone else in that church and it just seems sometimes as though we've no time for ourselves at all. I'm fed up to the neck!

<u>1967</u>

Sept. 19: At a meeting of the Executive Committee of the Missionary Society, I told them that I had joined the Suburban Women's Club and am resigning as an officer in the Missionary Society. I feel like a traitor but I am just

sick unto death of responsibility and the only way to get out is to leave entirely.

1968

Dec. 21: The largest church offering in 15 years I've been taking care of it.

GENE: (Autobiography)

In 1968 Dorothy was still financial secretary of the Delavan Avenue Baptist Church. I had been chairman of the board of deacons for two or three years. The church attendance had been stable or declining for several reasons: many of the former members had moved to the suburbs; Rev. Nowlan was not able to preach inspiring sermons and the area [around the church] was populated with black people who went to their own churches. All of these things bothered us. We did not think we were accomplishing anything there. Dorothy and I were trying to make up our minds about leaving the church and thought a good time would be the end of the year. I arranged to have Bob Weymouth elected chairman of the board of deacons and in early December Dorothy turned over her records to Kenneth Ratts to keep while we were on vacation.

We did not go back to the Delavan Avenue Church. We felt the best thing to do was to join another church where we could be more effective. We joined the Brighton Community Church. It was a young church and the opportunity to be a part of a younger group appealed to us.

DOROTHY: (Autobiography, 1998)

We joined the Brighton Community Church in 1969. It was a suburban church with many young families but we never enjoyed the same fellowship as we had at Delavan.

EDITOR

Although the Allberts left the Delavan Ave. Church, they did not end their wonderful friendships with the Delavan people which continued the rest of their lives. But they enlarged their social circles as they devoted more time to such activities as bowling, bridge and fishing. Unfortunately, Dorothy's health problems significantly limited her enjoyment of life.

DOROTHY: (Diary)

<u>1967</u>

April 22: I went to Surgery at about 1:00 and was back in my room at 2:30. Had anaesthetic and Dr. Hardner [the Urologist] said he treated quite a large ulcer in the bladder.

Oct. 30: I spent most of today just taking it easy. My Cystitis has got going again. It is so discouraging to have that to contend with all the time.

EDITOR

In the spring of 1967, Dr. Dayer was drafted for the Vietnam War. He and his family were stationed at Fort McPherson, Atlanta, Georgia for the next two years. In November, Dorothy drove to Atlanta with Roberta and the three children, where Roger met them after completing his basic training in San Antonio, Texas. Gene and Dorothy came to Atlanta for both Christmases. In March of 1969, they found a house for the Dayers to buy

on Woodbridge Avenue in Buffalo and then spent a lot of time that summer cleaning it for them to move in! Unfortunately, Dorothy's struggle with cystitis continued but she managed to enjoy somewhat limited activities, never knowing when it would flare up again.

EDITOR

In October, 1973 Eugene turned 65 which was the mandatory retirement age at Westinghouse. His colleagues organized a dinner celebration for Gene and promptly elected him to be President of the Westinghouse Veterans Organization.

DOROTHY (Diary)

<u>1972</u>

Aug. 7: It is 45 years now that Gene has worked at Westinghouse. They are making quite a bit of it- - - took his picture and gave him a tie tac with a diamond in it. He is so modest but very pleased.

<u>1973</u>

Sept. 18: All our plans now are zeroing in on our Departure Date—Oct. 26th.

Oct. 23: Tonight was Gene's Retirement Dinner and it was just lovely. About 150 people were there.

Oct. 24: This was Gene's last day at Westinghouse after more than 46 years!

GENE: (Autobiography)

My friends at Westinghouse made plans for a Retirement Party and had asked people to write letters that could be put in a book and presented at the dinner.

It was a great party and I was pleased that so many attended. Gene Ross, the manager of the group I was in, had made new assignments for all persons who had worked for me before I left. This was of interest to me.

We were able to leave Buffalo on our first long motor home trip on October 26, 1973.

EDITOR

In his response at the Retirement Dinner, Gene said: (Gene's Retirement Book) Retiring can be like graduating: there can be the graduation exercises with a speech on commencement. The retirement part means separation from many people I have known for some time. This I will miss ... I have had a good time for most of my years. The work was interesting; I have learned many things and the people were grand.

Now for the commencement part: Most of you know of our plans to take an extended trip, primarily in the southern part of USA. Dorothy, Mrs. A. to most of you, is quite a planner. This trip is probably her idea and I am pleased to be sold on the idea. Traveling is not new but traveling in a motor home is new. We will each learn some new things about living and about people.

EDITOR

Sometime after his retirement, one of Gene's engineers who had had moved to West Virginia, wrote Gene a long letter, describing Gene's influence on himself and others: (Hand-written, abridged letter in Gene's Retirement Book, date and author uncertain, but appears to be Tad Martin.)

"Dear Gene,

I wanted to tell you how much I have enjoyed working under your supervision. If I was sorry to leave my job, it was chiefly due to my belief that it will be hard if not impossible to find another person of your caliber to work for.

I wonder how much you realize your popularity amongst all the people in your section. The proof of my words can be found in the fact, that most of the fellows are trying to make extra effort in work, not for their own or company's sake, but for the fear of representing you personally. I have often admired your impartiality, your effort in helping individuals, and never for a moment losing temper or displaying dissatisfaction.

These last four years of work with you will always serve as an outstanding example of high human relationship and will guide me in my future efforts.

Thank you, Gene,"

EDITOR

And so, the 46 years at Westinghouse came to a happy conclusion, as Gene and Dorothy cheerfully set off in their motor home for points West and South.

CHAPTER V:

GENE AND DOROTHY Retirement Years, 1973-1987

A Taste of Luxury

EDITOR

The first decade of retirement was a happy and busy time for Gene and Dorothy, filled with travel, family celebrations, volunteer activities and an active social life. Their 50th wedding celebration in 1980 marked a high point in their lives together. During this period, most Americans experienced a dramatic rise in their standard of living, as did the Allberts. Inevitably however, as they grew older, many of their best friends died, moved away or became too ill to join them in former activities. Dorothy frequently advised her daughters: "Make younger friends"!

The Allberts continued to be closely involved with Roberta's family, which made it possible for her to take research trips, teach and write. Because "Dr. Roger" was frequently "on call" or in surgery, Nana and Boppa (as they now were known) would move into the Dayers' big, old house at 143 Woodbridge, and supervise the three young people while Roberta was out-of-town. In this way, they became almost second parents to the Dayer children, forging the closest of bonds. Boppa almost always appeared at the Dayers on Saturday morning with his leather suitcase full of tools, ready to fix whatever was broken. Gene had so much energy that Nana was happy for him to be busy and Roberta usually gave him his lunch on Saturday - - - the normal chicken noodle soup and grilled cheese sandwiches (with pickles for Boppa).

EUGENE: (Autobiography)

In our rented motor home, we traveled west ([in 1973], stopping in Peoria, Illinois to see Aunt Sadie and Topeka, Kansas, to see my brother Vernon. We visited Peggy's family in Englewood, Colorado and parked our motor home in their back yard for a month. We had Thanksgiving with the Clarkes and traveled around the area and visited many points of interest. A heavy snow fall made it possible to get pictures of the mountains from their back yard and of the snow on the motor home. We visited Dorothy's aunt, Edna Culp, in Raton and went on down to Albuquerque and then west to Kingman, Arizona. Here we turned north to Boulder Canyon. The view from the road as we came over the rise at the edge of the canyon was terrifying. The rough, brown rock walls made you feel like this was a picture of what hell must be like. We stopped at a viewing area and tried to absorb the scene. As I look back on it, I wonder what those people who built Hoover Dam must have thought of conquering such an environment. We went on over Hoover Dam and had a tour of the area where the water to the turbines divided into the various penstocks.

The next day we went on our way to Sunnyvale, California to visit Ruth and Roy and their family. We stayed there a month and had Christmas with them . . . The gas shortage due to the Arabs not selling oil to the States was a scare to us. We met Evelyn [Dorothy's half-sister] and George Meeks in San Francisco and drove to Point Reyes to see the whales and then on to a campground near Petaluma to spend the night. The next day we drove around the north end of the Bay to Vallejo to see Treva and Ray Grimes. We were able to get enough gas to leave Sunnyvale and then bought gasoline wherever we could.

We followed the Rio Grande River to Big Bend Park and spent several days there ... The next day we left for San Antonio. Here we took a tour around the city and spent some time at the Alamo ... In New Orleans, we had a tour of the city and visited the French Quarter. We picked up mail at Mobile, Alabama and went to see the Bellingrath Gardens; then to Dauphin Island camp ground to spend the night. This was memorable because there was a place to fish and a rooster that crowed at four a.m. We continued east along the Gulf coast. Just before we reached Florida there is a concrete pier. I fished there and caught four whiting fish. When I returned to the motorhome, I found Dorothy had baked a cake ... we started for St. Petersburg where Balls lived, staying in St. Petersburg about a month. We went around the south end of Florida, visiting many of the people we knew when they lived in Buffalo. We were gone about five and a half months and had determined the motorhome was the way to travel. We had driven 11,368 miles ....

EDITOR

After President Lyndon B. Johnson, distraught by popular opposition to the Vietnam war, announced in the spring of 1968 that he would not seek re-election in the fall, Richard Nixon was elected President in November,1968, defeating the Democratic candidate, Hubert Humphrey. Nixon was re-elected in 1972, after successfully ending the Vietnam War and establishing diplomatic relations with Communist China. However, in 1974, the Watergate Crisis led to Nixon's downfall, forcing him to resign. Since the Vice-President, Spiro Agnew, already had resigned in a political scandal, the Speaker of the House of Representatives, Gerald Ford, became President, and completed Nixon's term. But in the election of 1976, Governor Jimmy Carter, the Democratic candidate from Georgia, defeated President Ford, partly because he had pardoned Richard Nixon. The Allberts showed little interest in politics during their early retirement, focusing instead on travel and family.

EUGENE: (Autobiography)

In the spring of 1975, Dorothy and I went to a recreation vehicle show (RV) and became interested in purchasing a motor home. We found one with most of the features we wanted and at a price we could afford. It was a Rockwood, 20-foot-long, transmission air conditioned on the engine, and all of the furnishings we needed. We were able to buy this for $10,000. We later added a 120-volt air conditioner for the living quarters for $500. In April, we made our first trip with the motorhome to Monroeville, Pa., to show the Robinsons our purchase. The trip went well. Now we were ready to take a longer trip.

EDITOR

In the next few years, the Allberts took many trips in their Motor Home, visiting friends and relatives all over the United States and having a wonderful time - - - so much so that by the end of their travels, they had visited all 48 contiguous states, plus Hawaii.

EUGENE: (Autobiography)

The first summer, 1974, of my retirement, gave me an opportunity to do something at Camp Vick and so I offered to act as a counselor of junior boys for ten days. This went off quite well. In July 1977, I was the Craft Director at Camp Vick for five weeks. I tried to have the children use pieces of wood to make small items and use water base paints to make fancy bottles, and use plywood panels and macaroni to make plaques. I lived in the motor home and enjoyed the privacy it gave me. After dinner, I often took a canoe and anyone who wanted to go fishing on the pond. It was quiet and restful after a day with the children.

The latter part of March, 1978, I started working for the Buffalo Electric Co., doing drafting, making electric wiring diagrams and other drawings required. This was on a part time basis as they had work and as I had time. This continued with Buffalo Electric until November 1983 John Burgio had asked Ed Laughlin [at Westinghouse] about someone who could make drawings; Ed recommended me. John went to Fishback &

Moore and most of the work went with him. He asked me to do their work and at times I worked for both of the companies. I received my last check on September 15, 1987. The total was about $22,000 earned by the time we left Buffalo for California. I could work at home or at their plants as it suited me and the people with whom I worked were very pleasant and appreciated my work.

Each of us was in bowling leagues and I think this was the first of three years that I was secretary of the Amherst Senior Center Bowling League. This involved much work. There were about thirty teams of four bowlers each.

The Camera Club had a print exhibit each spring and I was in charge of this in 1985. We had learned to make mats for our prints and I had tools to cut these. I invited any members who wanted to make their mats to come to our house and we would do this together. Our studio room was just the place for such activities. Most of the mats on my enlargements are home made. The exhibit was a success and the Senior Center asked us to set it up in their auditorium for a month. I think I received two ribbons for the pictures I submitted.

Dorothy was very much involved in a project, which began in the summer of 1974 and lasted until December of 1975. Our friends, Donald and Edith Smith, [from Delavan Ave. church] were having a very hard time. Donald was badly afflicted with Parkinson's disease and Edith was having an eye problem. Neither of them could drive so Dorothy began taking Edith to the doctor. Don became very bad, was hospitalized and died in August,

1974. All of this involved many business trips for Edith and Dorothy drove her. Her only close relatives were in Canada [she was a Canadian Citizen] and she badly needed active help and moral support. Her eyesight became so bad that Dorothy was appointed her Power of Attorney. Her health failed too and there were many trips to the doctor and hospital. Finally, she went into a nursing home and in the fall of 1975, we took her to Canada to live. [in a Nursing Home near her nephew]. Her furniture was all in the house in Buffalo and we had the job first of sorting through her clothes and personal possessions before she moved, and afterward we sold some of the furniture for her. We kept a strict account of all money received and turned it over to her nephew. She seemed very grateful for our help and gave us a number of her beautiful things.

EDITOR

From the above account and from what follows in Dorothy's diary, one can see that Gene and Dorothy learned a valuable lesson about aging. When the time came that they could no longer manage their own house, they chose to live in a retirement community where they would not depend on children or friends to meet their needs. Their sad and frustrating experience with Grandma Allbert convinced them that it was preferable to be on your own in a retirement community, rather than living in someone else's home. Multiple entries in Dorothy's diary make clear not only how much she suffered emotionally from her experience with her friend

Edith, but how much she resented all the time spent taking care of her in 1975. I quote A Few Examples.

DOROTHY: (Diary)

<u>1975</u>

Sept. 16: I am so upset about Edith. She has sure turned out to be a headache!

Sept. 24: We had an appointment with Edith's lawyer this morning and he is going to try to do something about getting the house sold.

Sept. 29: We took Edith to Dr. Schopp to be told he can't do anymore for her eyes and she is blind. <u>Sad, Sad, Sad.</u>

Oct. 2: Tonight Don Flett called with joyful news. There is a place at the Retirement home in Canada for Edie and a possibility of selling the house.

Oct. 7: I was tired and somewhat dispirited today. It is so hard to break up someone's home. I took some things she wanted given to the Thrift Store and got her new dark glasses and took them down to her. She seemed pleased with them.

Oct. 23: We went to Edith's and packed some more after bowling.

Dec. 29: Left home in Motor Home for Florida.

EDITOR

In the late '70s, Dorothy's health problems continued to limit her activities and affect the quality of their lives. The interstitial cystitis continued and in addition, Dorothy suffered two serious falls while traveling. One resulted in a broken shoulder and the second a broken wrist. Nonetheless, she and Gene managed to travel thousands of miles in their motor home: Big trips involved Florida and California; smaller trips to New England and the Adirondacks, where they not only "saw the sights" but visited friends and relatives without feeling that they were infringing on their hospitality.

EUGENE: (Autobiography)

The middle of June, 1977, we went to North Otto [south of Buffalo] to see Jim and Eva Ball for two days and a night. When we returned home, and were unloading the motor home Dorothy tripped and fell from the door and broke her shoulder. It was very painful and had to be operated on to add a steel plate to hold the parts together. She was in the hospital for six days and stayed at Bobbi's for about a month. After some therapy, she regained most of the original movement of her arm, except she could not raise it as high as before.

DOROTHY: (Diary)

<u>1977</u>

June 17: The last 24 hours have been a nightmare of ambulance, x-rays, pain, sweat and anesthetic but my arm is fixed up and now all it needs is time to get better.

June 19: I've felt quite chipper all day today and have had a lot of company which I enjoy but is very tiring.

June 22: I had x-rays made of my arm yesterday and it looked so good the doctor released me and I have come to Dayers' home to recuperate.

June 25: A busy Saturday. The kids had their music lessons this a.m. and I had my hair done this afternoon. Marge K[ennedy, Roger's sister] and Grandma Dayer had supper with us but tonight everyone was out.

June 26: A beautiful Summer Sunday. Larry graduated from Bennett Hi and later there was a lovely party here for him---21 people of all ages. I went down for a while. Gene left after the graduation to take up his summer duties at Camp Vick, so he will be gone until next Saturday.

July 7: Bobbi and I went to my house and got beds made up for Peggy and her family. They arrived about 9:30 tonight. We had some refreshments and then Bobbi showed them to our house.

July 8: Peggy, John and 3 children had a good night of rest and breakfast at our house and came over here about noon. This afternoon they all went to Art Park [a nearby, outdoor cultural center in Lewiston, NY]. Gene came home and we all, including Grandma [Dayer] had a delicious lasagna dinner.

July 24: For the first time in six weeks I got a dress and stockings on and went to church. Quite a few people welcomed me back. We had lunch at home and Gene left again. Bobbi came over for a while. It seems so lifeless here after the hustle and bustle at her home.

EDITOR

In 1978, Dorothy and Gene made two major trips in their Motor Home: First to Florida from January until mid-March; then on Oct. 31st, they began a trip to the West, which lasted until mid-March 1979. One of the ways they broke up their weeks of travel was to stop on the way to visit friends. One cannot but be impressed with the complicated planning involved in all the arrangements for these trips. Between January and March, as they made their way south, they visited friends from Turtle Creek, Westinghouse, and Delavan Ave. Church. In the fall, they started West, where they would celebrate Thanksgiving with Ruthie's family in Los Altos Hills, and Christmas with Peggy in Denver.

DOROTHY: (Diary)

<u>1978</u>

Nov. 3: We got to Sally Cooper's [Aunt Sadie's daughter] home in Peoria about 2:30 and backed in to the Driveway and plugged in [for electricity]. When she came home from work we all went out to eat. She is so nice and makes us feel so welcome.

Nov. 5: This evening there was a family dinner but there were only 6 of us tonight and there used to be such a crowd. It was nice though.

Nov. 7: We stopped in Independence, Mo. And visited the Truman Library and Museum. It was very interesting. We reached Vernon & Portla's home near Topeka, Kansas.

Nov. 9: We drove over 400 miles as far as Limon, Col. The weather is turning cold and snowy so we are glad we aren't very far from our destination in Denver.

Nov. 10: We were at Peggy's home by 10:30. She had a holiday from work today and we've all had a good time visiting together.

Nov. 12: This has been a really pleasant day. We 4 adults drove Mary Ellen back to Boulder [U. of Colorado where she went to college] and had a restaurant lunch. This afternoon we played Racko and Dominoes with Mark, Katie and Stephanie. Those two "little girls" 11 and 14, are just delightful. After dinner, we played Dominoes with Peggy.

Nov. 17: We drove up to Evergreen [Colorado] to visit Kenneth [Gene's brother] and Beth. They gave us a delicious dinner and we visited and watched TV until after 10:00.

Nov. 19: We borrowed luggage from Clarkes to use to fly out to Calif.

Nov. 20: Ruth met us and drove us to her lovely new home in Los Altos Hills.

Nov. 22: A busy day! Phyllis arrived home from Berkeley and Roy's parents came from Medford, OR and are at his sister's.

Nov. 23: A fantastic Thanksgiving. I helped Ruth by ironing linen, polishing silver, etc. There were 14 of us for a wonderful Turkey dinner and day together.

Nov. 26: Another big day. We went to the Menlo Park Presbyterian Church with Ruth, Roy and David. We were all invited to Roy's sister's home for <u>another</u> big dinner and later Ruth, Mildred [Roy's mother] and I shopped. I am getting a lot of Christmas shopping done and it is time!

Dec. 2: We were up early to get packed for our trip to San Francisco on the Commuter's train. It is fun! Evelyn and George met us in San Bruno and we've spent the day eating and visiting. Evelyn is lively only she talks one up the wall!

Dec. 3: This has been another beautiful day. We went to the <u>very</u> ultra-swank Crown Room in the Fairmount Hotel for an elegant Brunch. The view up there was magnificent. George took us for a nice ride after that.

Dec. 10: We went up in the hills and chopped down a gorgeous Christmas tree. Gene & Roy worked most of the evening setting it up and we had Pizza for supper and watched "The Gathering" on T.V.

Dec. 14: Busy all morning packing to go back to Denver. Our stay with the Rogers has been just wonderful. The trip was a little rough but Peggy met us and we are back in our little Motor Home again tonight.

Dec. 24: This has been a beautiful warm day. Peggy had us in for a family breakfast, then Gene and I went to a Baptist church nearby. This afternoon Steffi and I baked some cookies and tonight we all went to Christmas Eve service at a Catholic Church, then opened a few gifts and had refreshments.

Dec. 25: This has been a lovely Christmas. There were presents galore for everyone and about 3:00 we had a delicious dinner. We provided the ham for it.

Dec. 31: The last day of 1978. We went to church with Peg & Steffi. This afternoon I made some more snacks and some fudge for them and we had a pleasant dinner. This is their 23rd wedding anniversary.

<u>1979</u>

Jan. 1: Left Clarke's about 10:30 and drove to Raton, New Mexico. It is very cold but we have a place in a good Camp Ground with electricity.

Jan. 4: Another day of driving and we make it to Tucson, Ariz. By mid-afternoon. We are quite tired after our 4 days of traveling and it will be nice to stay here for a while.

Jan. 9: Today, Elizabeth Bernard Wheeler whom we knew in Raton, N.M. over 60 years ago came and took us to lunch to the De Grana Museum and then insisted we bring the Motor Home out to their place at Marana, Arizona.

Jan. 10: We had such a great visit with the Wheelers and with Mildred Canfield who was my <u>very</u> first girlfriend. She lives near them.

Jan. 22: We made reservations to go up to the Grand Canyon on a Bus trip Thursday and Friday. We moved in to Tempe and are paying $10.00 a night!

Jan. 25-26: All bright and bushy tailed for our trip but it has turned out very disappointing. Weather so bad we can hardly see the Canyon. The other people on the trip were nice and it would have been great. Anyway, we are back safely.

Jan. 31: We said a fond good-by to our good friends and drove as far as El Paso, Texas. It is warmer here.

Feb. 5: In to Del Rio but mail still not there. What a disappointment.

Feb. 6: <u>Finally</u> the sun shone and the mail came with letters from Bobbi, Bette R. & Ethel Richards [an old friend from Turtle Creek]. So we got going and drove clear over on the Coast to Padre Island.

Feb. 7: There is such a cold wind here that we drove on up to Port Arkansas and at last Gene caught a little Whiting.

Feb. 9: We drove to Galveston State Park today.

Feb. 11: After going to church and having our dinner, I fell on the sidewalk and broke my wrist!

Feb. 12: Today has seemed like a re-play of a bad dream. My wrist was badly injured and required surgery and I'm in St. Mary's hospital. Everyone is being very nice to me and Gene has a place to park nearby.

Feb. 13: I've had an I.V. in my right arm all day so have been almost helpless. Gene has done nursing duty and been so kind and tonight they took out the IV so now I can get out of bed at least.

Feb. 14: Life in the hospital is interesting but tiresome. I am in a room with 2 other women. Today has been quite nice and Gene went fishing for a while.

Feb. 17: A wet, cold day. I got out of the hospital right after lunch and into the Motor Home again.

Feb. 20: A rather bad day. Gene was so grouchy and I had a hysterical spell and cried and cried. This afternoon we went to Pirate's Beach and Gene did our laundry.

Feb. 22: My arm is badly swollen and one wound is draining so we are back at the island (Galveston) till next Tues.

Feb. 27: Dr. J. said arm much better but still not ready for cast. Thank Goodness we have the TV!

March 2: Today has been Red Letter in two respects: I had my hair done at 10:00 and that makes me look and feel a lot better. Then this afternoon I got the cast on my arm at last.

March 5: The doctor gave us permission to leave and after many errands we got started and drove as far as Lafayette, LA.

March 8: We continued our journey and were in Arden, NC. at the home of Ruth and Bill Roberts [Westinghouse friends] by mid-afternoon. It seems so good to see them again and they have a lovely new home in a beautiful area.

March 9: It is just great to have a rest from traveling and to see our friends again.

March 11: We said goodbye to our friends and left about 10 am and got almost to Lexington, KY.

March 12: The weather was great, the road was dry, we got an early start and drove all the way home-over 500 miles. We got to Dayers in time to eat with Bobbi and the children. Larry is home from college.

March 13: How wonderful to be in our own pleasant home again. I rested most of the day. Bobbi invited us over for dinner. Dr. [Roger] just got back from Florida. He wants me to see Dr. Sterman [an Orthopedic Surgeon] at once.

March 14: Went to see Dr. Sterman. He took my cast off, made more x-rays and sent me right off to the hospital again. He is going to do my arm over. I sure feel discouraged!

March 15: I have a nice room and a pleasant roommate and had my arm done again this afternoon. Apparently, the setting had slipped and there was also a lot more pus in the arm. Anyway, it is done again.

March 20: Tonight I am home again!

March 21: So wonderful to be home! Bobbi came for lunch today and she said Dr. Sterman told Roger he was delighted with the x-rays that were taken yesterday.

EDITOR

After having such a terrible experience with the broken wrist, Gene and Dorothy lost their appetite for long trips in the Motor Home. They sold the Motor Home to Bill and Ruth Roberts (Westinghouse friends) in 1980.

In March 1979, a very happy development occurred when TV producer, Rick Kellman, selected Gene and Dorothy to be one of the couples to be featured in a TV series called: "Marriage Buffalo Style". Since they had been married almost 50 years, Mr. Kellman chose them as an example of a long-lasting marriage.

DOROTHY: (Diary)

1979

March 27: Rich Kellman from TV Channel 2, called and is going to interview us for a TV series on marriage. Exciting!

April 5: I feel so much happier when I get away from the house a while so today we went out to the Bowling Lanes and Gene bowled and I visited some with the bowlers I know.

April 9: This broken wrist has caused me the most inactivity and boredom I've ever experienced, but I guess it will end sometime.

April 11: Rich Kellman and a photographer from Channel 2 were here for 2 ½ hours interviewing us and taking pictures. They were so nice and we are excited about being on TV.

April 12: I went to the Church Women's Society meeting last night and after such a big day yesterday I've been completely blotto today. Iris [Henderson} called and drafted me to be President of Suburban Women's Club next year! Yipes!

May 9: The TV series "Marriage Buffalo Style" is on this week and is very good.

May 12: Tonight Rick showed the whole series on another program and we were on again at 11:00 pm.

May 13: Mother's Day. So many compliments we received at church. Dayers took us to Cherry Hill [Golf Club in Canada] for dinner.

EDITOR

In his interview, Rich Kellman asked the Allberts how they explained the success of their long marriage. Dorothy replied: "There are good times and bad times; ups and downs, and you just have to persevere." It was a wonderful explanation.

In 1980, the Allberts' busy and happy life continued to be filled with bridge, bowling, camera club, travel and church activities. They began planning for their 50th wedding anniversary. One of the happiest developments for Dorothy was that she finally had her own car!

DOROTHY: (Diary)

1980

Jan. 4: I am to have a new ring for our Golden Anniversary year and today after Gene went to the Westinghouse Retiree's lunch we picked it out. I'm very pleased with it.

May 21: Gene went out and brought home our new car and he is keeping the [Ford] LTD for me!!!

June 10: This was Suburban Club Installation Luncheon at Brookfield Country Club. Everything went just beautifully. There were 76 women there. Gene took pictures for us and I was given a standing ovation! I was thrilled! I feel so good about my year [as President] but it is nice to have it over. June 29: **OUR 50TH WEDDING ANNIVERSARY**: was such a special time! I have to give it a special page. This week-end there are eight of us at our house---14 over at Dayers' and 6 dear friends, Clifford & Rhoda Allen, Ethel Richard, Al, Betty and Bobbie Robinson at a Motel. All 28 showed up at church and we filled the 4 pews reserved for us.

The Reception [at church] this afternoon was wonderful beyond words---about 150 people were there---the room was beautifully decorated. There was a wonderful cake and a Program, which the girls had planned and which was just wonderful.

There have been many gifts and a deluge of beautiful cards and tonight the Dayers had a Buffet for family, out-of-town guests and some friends of theirs who weren't at the reception. Truly a Golden Day. Tomorrow is the actual anniversary date.

EUGENE: (Autobiography) Account of 50th Anniversary:

Ruth and Roy and all nine cousins stayed at the Dayers. The young people had a wonderful time becoming really acquainted. John III was in the Marines in Japan and could not attend.

On June 30th about 20 of us went to Station WGR and Rich Kellman showed the TV program, "Marriage Buffalo Style", in which we had been a part. That evening Bobbi and Roger hosted a dinner party for the family and out of town guests at the Cherry Hill Country Club in Canada. The next day people began to depart. It was a full week until the last had gone. It will always be a cherished memory as one of our happiest times in our lives.

EDITOR

Despite their busy and happy lives, Dorothy and Gene were beginning to feel conscious of their advancing years as their friends continued to die off. They bought burial plots in Forest Lawn Cemetery in order to prepare for "the inevitable'. In the summer of 1981, Dorothy flew to California and Denver while Gene counseled at Camp Vick.

DOROTHY: (Diary)

1981

May 26: So our happy lives go on day after day--- "Sunrise, Sunset, swiftly flow the years."

June 30: The trip to California was 6 hours long but it was a beautiful day and I was interested in identifying the States as we flew over them. Ruth and Phyllis were at the Airport in San Francisco to meet me.

July 3: Ruth, Roy and I drove to Medford, Oregon for a visit with Roy's parents.

July 23: I arrived in Denver about 6:30 and dear Peggy was there to meet me. It was breathlessly hot!

July 31: My visit out west is over and I'm home again. It was all just about perfect and the time just passed all too quickly but I'm still just so happy to be home again.

<u>1982</u>

June 24: Gene preparing for month at Camp Vick. His energy is just beyond normal comprehension! Not easy to live with and impossible to match!

June 30: Gene to Camp Vick. I'm staring at 10 lonely days.

July 3: I've spent a lot of time composing a letter to Anne Morrow Lindbergh. I've been so fascinated with her biographical books this Spring and yesterday I read another of her early books: "The Steep Ascent" and I've always admired her so much and have been toying with the idea of writing her for years.

EDITOR:

Anne Morrow Lindbergh was a well-known writer, not only for her books but also because she was the wife of Charles Lindbergh, the famous aviator, who flew solo over the Atlantic Ocean in 1929. After their marriage in 1927, Anne also became an aviator and accompanied her husband on his many adventurous flights. The Lindberghs became the first to fly from Africa to South America. The young couple suffered the terrible and heavily publicized kidnapping of their child in 1932.

The subsequent, feverish press coverage led them to seek seclusion by living abroad for many years.

Dorothy did write a long letter to Ms. Lindbergh, which she concluded with the comment: "How many times you must have thought 'they also serve who only stand and wait'. Your description of those flights has been a refresher course in geography. . . I feel better educated because I have read your books." Unfortunately, Dorothy never received a response to this letter.

For the Allberts, the big event in 1982 was their trip to Hawaii. It was by far the most luxurious trip they had ever enjoyed! Since the Roy Rogers were at their condo in Kauai, Gene and Dorothy visited them as well. They traveled by way of Denver, where they stayed with the Clarkes a few days and saw all of the Denver grandchildren.

DOROTHY: (Diary)

1982

Aug. 17: [Hawaii] We have a lovely place to stay- - - a Penthouse on the 44th floor with a nice balcony (lanai) where we can look down on city traffic and the tops of many other buildings and a good view of Diamond Head.

Aug. 19: I was so glad to get away from hot, busy Honolulu and take the short plane trip over to Kauai where Ruth and Roy were waiting for us with a beautiful lei for me and it was great to go back to their beautiful condo and have a nice lunch with them and Phyllis and

David. . . . This place is really a tropical Paradise and the living is lush beyond anything we've ever known.

Aug. 23: Caught the inter-island plane for Maui. We are delighted with our place here.

Aug. 28: We have a perfectly beautiful place to stay here too---an apartment in a beautiful hotel-the Kona Lagoon.

Aug. 29: Our very last day in Hawaii. And it has been almost perfect. . . I had persuaded Gene that a trip to Hawaii wouldn't be complete without a Luau. We watched them take the roasted pig out of the pit and heard the story of the ceremony . . . The music began and about 250 people were served a regular Hawaiian food buffet of which the roast pork was one of the main features. I went lightly on the food as so much of it was new and unknown but thoroughly enjoyed the Polynesian show. So now our "visit in Paradise" is over, but we still have our week in Ruth & Roy's home, [in Los Altos Hills] to enjoy.

Oct. 2: Being alone for a while restores my soul.

1983

June 25: Gene said he gets tired sooner than he used to and his Allergy is so bad. I feel so well and am probably happier and contented with my life than I've ever been. These are really our "golden years."

Aug. 14: Sunday and my 73d birthday. I just can't believe I'm that old! . . . I feel so blessed to be as well as I am and in my right mind. Sometimes I wonder if the unhappy years I had in my early life are being made up to me in my "later years". Anyway, I feel well compensated and very thankful!

Sept. 10: Balls' cottage [in Canada]: About 20 [Delavan Ave. group] came by noon and we had a wonderful meal as we always do. We were saddened though by the announcement that Balls probably won't be there next year so this will be the last Delavan picnic. Several of the people are in poor health.

EDITOR

Unfortunately, in 1984, Dorothy decided to begin a Weight Watchers' program which may have been instrumental in the onset of rheumatoid arthritis and serious depression.

DOROTHY: (Diary)

1984

April 12: Gene informed me this morning that he is considering taking the job of Ass't Manager at Camp Vick which would mean he'd be giving even more time and thought to it than he already does. Well, I just rebelled at last and told him, in essence, that he had to choose between Camp Vick and me. Se he called Syracuse and told them he couldn't do it!

April 13: I'm in a very low and depressed frame of mind. I just feel as though I might as well be dead for all it would matter.

April 15. I'm just so depressed I feel like ending it all.

April 30: Still depressed. Gene is just so energetic and so exuberant all the time and completely unmindful of how lonely and depressed I am.

May 2: I'm trying to analyze my depression and hopefully conquer it. Perhaps some of it is withdrawal pangs due to dieting when I love food so.

May 7: I've been deep in the Slough of Depression again all day and I <u>must</u> pull myself out- - - no one else is going to! I keep having suicidal thoughts.

June 30: Our 54th wedding anniversary. It doesn't seem possible, but life seems great still.

Aug. 1: For some reason my legs are so sore today that it is painful to walk.

Aug. 2: Dr. Roger thinks my Weight Watcher's diet is giving me Gout and that I should resume a more normal diet. Anyway, I've lost at least 15 pounds (least weight in 20 years).

Oct. 7: Didn't get dressed all day. Bobbi came over and ironed a lot of Gene's shirts.

Oct. 9: Gene is helping with housework but <u>hates</u> to cook.

Oct. 13: Dr. Marine [a prominent Rheumatologist and a close friend of the Dayers] thinks I have Rheumatoid Arthritis.

Dec. 27: To California; Ruth and Roy welcomed us very warmly.

Dec. 30: Peggy arrived from Denver. We are all <u>so</u> happy to be together.

1985

Jan. 1: A wonderful thing to be with two of our daughters on New Year's Day. Peggy and I watched and very much enjoyed the Rose Bowl Parade.

Jan. 6. Tonight, Gene, Phyllis [Rogers] and I watched the first episode of "The Thorn Birds". It was excellent.

Jan. 11: Bobbi and Roger E. & Cindy were at the Air Port to meet us. I have come home feeling better than when I left. Hope I can keep that way and continue improving.

Jan. 28: Nice not to feel so depressed.

Feb. 5: Gene was "up and off" early to get more food supplies to the Council [of Churches] House. If he were paid even a minimum wage for all the volunteer work he has given through the years we'd be millionaires! But he never seems to tire or get discouraged---though sometimes he gets disgusted.

May 1: Gene went out to the Williamsville Library this morning and got the Print Show set up. He won two ribbons on his pictures in the judging. I'm so glad because he is so interested in photography and gives it so much time and effort.

May 21: My legs are so sore it was torture going up and down the basement stairs.

June 3: Socializing really takes the starch out of me.

June 30: This was our 55th wedding anniversary and Bobbi went to church with us and had flowers in our honor and after church she and Dr. took us to dinner at the Glen Iris Inn in Letchworth Park. It was a beautiful trip and a delicious dinner. The 3 girls gave us a beautiful large leather-bound Family Bible. How blessed we are!

July 18: I seem to love my girls more all the time.

July 28: A beautiful but for me a very quiet Sunday. I've had a lot of pain in my hands and arms and my shoulders are very stiff. Gene helped me get dressed for church and he left right after lunch for his last week at Camp Vick for this year.

EDITOR

Dorothy's spirits were lifted when she and Gene took a wonderful trip to the Canadian Rocky Mountains, in August. They took a bus to Toronto and flew from there to Vancouver. The itinerary featured a visit to the Butchart Gardens in Victoria, and an overnight train trip to Lake Louise.

DOROTHY: (Diary)

1985

Aug. 14: Today is my 75th birthday and to spend it in the Canadian Rockies is a dream realized ... We ate at the Chateau Lake Louise where we will spend tomorrow and tomorrow night. The scenery here is breathtaking and I'm so happy. This will surely be one of my most memorable birthdays.

Aug. 18: To Banff, which I believe is the most beautiful place of all. We are staying at Banff Lodge, a building built for millionaires. This trip is the most luxurious one we've ever had.

Aug. 19: This is the last day of our tour and it has been one of the pleasantest yet. The first thing this morning we were driven up to Sulphur Mountain and had a wonderful ride in a gondola up, up & up to where we could see the tops of many surrounding peaks- - - a beautiful sight . . . saw the helicopter arrive with Prince Phillip and his retinue.

Sept. 13: Balls' cottage in Canada. "We women walked over to Hills' [other Delavan friends] for a few minutes and just visited together. We all felt a little saddened by the obvious changes Time brings and we said" good by" to Balls, as they will soon be going back to Florida.

EDITOR:

Since Dorothy continued to suffer from disabling pain, she and Gene began to consider moving. Their daughter Ruth had suggested that they live in California. In 1986, they had an ideal opportunity to try living temporarily in the Villa Serena Retirement Center in Santa Clara, only a few miles from the Rogers.

DOROTHY: (Diary)

1986

Jan.30: To California to "house-sit" Ruth & Roy's house, while they are in Australia and New Zealand.

March 5: To Denver: Mary Ellen Clarke pregnant.

March 10: To Buffalo.

April 1: I've felt just terrible all day and am so discouraged. It is just so hard to do the simplest things.

With Gene's help I got two loads of laundry done but I only made one trip to the basement. I just <u>hate</u> being so useless and things are <u>not</u> improving, I'm sad to say... Ruthie called... She wants to have us come out again soon after Christmas and look at places for us to live... they want us to take part In The Choice. I Think They Are Very Considerate and I Won't need to worry about moving for a long time, which is a relief.

EDITOR:

Dorothy's continuing pain convinced the Allberts that a change in living location was necessary, so they began preparing.

DOROTHY: (Diary)

<u>1986</u>

April 25: Gene cleaned up his canoe and put it on the car to take it out and give it to Camp Vick, so that will be one possession disposed of.

Aug. 10: About 9 tonight we had the great news that our first great-grandchild is here. He is Thomas Clarke Ward and all is well.

Aug. 19: Bobbi did ironing again.

Aug. 20: My hands are so sore I can hardly use them.

Aug. 30: Gene left early today to spend the day at Camp Vick. He won't be going there many more times and has given up his job as Property Committee head.

Sept. 4: Blood tests showed anemia.

Sept. 23: I managed to cook dinner for the first time in two weeks.

Sept. 30: Gene has made the arrangements for me to fly to Calif. On Nov. 1st.

Oct. 8: Now Gene is having trouble with his stomach.

EDITOR

In October both Gene and Dorothy experienced significant health problems, necessitating many tests and doctor appointments. Gene had developed a stomach ulcer. Thus they became convinced they should move to a warmer climate. They had arranged to rent an apartment at the Villa Serena for three months, a place which had been recommended by Ruth's friends. They asked Vernon (Gene's brother) to come to Buffalo to drive their car and many possessions out to California, while Dorothy would fly out later.

DOROTHY: (Diary)

1986

Oct. 22: We are taking so much stuff (to California) it is a real challenge to get it all in the car.

Oct. 23: Gene and Vernon got off before 7:00 with a heavily loaded car . . . Bobbi spent the night.

Oct. 30: Dr. Marine said definitely Rheumatoid Arthritis.

Nov. 1: Betty Robinson died. Flew to California.

Nov. 11: I have felt much happier and less anxious than I did last night. I think God will show us what is the best thing for us to do.

Nov. 12: Saw Villa Serena. We think this is just what we want. At least we'll try it for Jan., Feb. and March.

1987

Feb. 24: I feel so satisfied with our way of life here- - - Gene spends so much more time with me and I like that.

March 9: Gene worked in Library [at Villa Serena].

March 18: Went to exercise class this morning and Gene went to the writing class this afternoon . . . We went to the Manager's office and talked about our plans and she showed us a nice apartment in Building 1 that she said she would try to save for us.

March 24: It is so great not to have housework to do.

April 22: John and Margaret Wright {new friends] called on us from Baptist Church. We think we will join.

EDITOR

Gene and Dorothy returned to Buffalo, determined to sell their house and move to California. They began distributing most of their possessions among children and friends.

DOROTHY: (Diary)

1987

June: House on the market.

July 9: Peggy left for Denver with a "well-loaded car".

Sept. 3: Well this is the day I've been waiting almost three months to record. We sold the house tonight!

Sept. 22: Packing furniture to go to California. Moved over to Dayers.

Sept. 24: It makes me feel sad to break up our lovely home but I am sure it is time it was done.

Sept. 27: The parting is hard.

Sept. 28: Bobbi took us to the plane and Ruthie met us in San Francisco.

Oct. 1: Moved into Villa Serena.

Nov. 24: The walker helps me so much. I can walk <u>almost</u> normally with it and the soreness in my legs seems to be abating somewhat.

Dec. 7: …the sunshine was pouring in which made things more cheerful. Maria, the maid, was here and cleaned the apartment. How nice it is to have the housework done.

EDITOR

And so Gene and Dorothy ended their forty years living in Buffalo, always courageously facing forward.

GENE AND DOROTHY, 1988-2000:

CHAPTER VI:

Life at the Villa Serena

Final Years

EDITOR

The first few years at the Villa Serena were filled with travel and happy times for Gene and Dorothy, as their grandchildren began to marry and produce great-grandchildren. Each summer they would return to Buffalo for an extended stay at the Dayers' house, which enabled them to visit with many of their long-time Buffalo friends.

Ruth and Roy Rogers' family organized wonderful celebrations for the 60th and 65th wedding anniversaries, to which most of the Allbert family came, from all parts of the country. And Gene assumed several new responsibilities as well as developing new interests.

Sadly, however, Dorothy's health deteriorated further, as she developed macular degeneration of the eyes, a condition which severely limited her ability to read. Rather than keeping a day-by-day diary in 1988, Dorothy decided instead to keep a monthly summary, writing longer accounts of special events. She wrote: "Our lives are not as event-filled as they used to be, but we still find it interesting day-by-day." Since traditionally, the Rogers family travelled to Hawaii to celebrate Christmas and New Year's, Gene and Dorothy took care of their house in Los Altos Hills while they were away.

DOROTHY: (Diary)

1988

There was a business meeting here early in the month and Gene was unanimously elected Chairman of the Residents' Council. The Villa plans many interesting things to do and trips to make which too few of the residents take advantage of. On Jan. 10 we went to an interesting Museum and Restaurant called "The Flying Lady", which was fun and on Jan. 29 we went to the Oakland Museum, which was very interesting, though tiring for me.

The monthly birthday party was celebrated and Gene took pictures. The ones that are good of people, he gives them and usually receives repeat orders. He is much in demand to take pictures and he enjoys it.

I don't do very much and yet the time passes quickly. I am stiff and in some degree of pain all the time and can take unlimited rest---and do. I do play bridge some in the evenings . . . We have joined the First Baptist Church of Santa Clara so we are church members again. I have been a member of six Baptist churches in my lifetime and Gene has belonged to five.

EUGENE: (Autobiography)

[After moving into our apartment at the Villa], I found that the baseboards in our hall had not been replaced. This disturbed Dorothy to no end. In fact, I thought I should do something about it. Management offered no help. The next thing to do was to get my tools and some baseboard material and nail it in place. Soon I was off the hook and ready to put the books back in the shelves in the library. We had a maintenance man named Tony. He bolted the shelves to the wall and then I could spend my spare time dusting, arranging and shelving books.

Dorothy started to use a walker in November, 1987. . . We continued to make friends here and take part in the activities. I think Ruth thought we would find things dull for us, but we found so much to do that we did not go to the Senior Center which she suggested. . . . The Manager asked us to form a Residents' Council. I was elected as Chairman and wrote a statement of purpose and a list of officers we would need to start the Council. . . . I have written a "History of Villa Serena, A Retirement Community", dated January, 1996.

I had been attending a writing class, which was given by the Santa Clara Adult Education Department and taught by Ann Thompson.

I had wondered what part I might play in the church we had joined. I learned they had a small food shelf program and it seemed to be like an orphan. There was no system of buying food, nor a list of what should be stocked. I went shopping with the person who bought the food and found I had a place where I could function well. It was not long before I bought, stocked and packed the food for the secretary to give to those in need.

EDITOR

On July 5, 1988, Gene and Dorothy flew to Buffalo, where granddaughter Cindy Dayer was to be married to Stephen Erb on July 30th. They were able to visit many old friends; play bridge, go to Camera Club, the Brighton Church, Westinghouse Veterans' luncheon, fish, etc. On July 28th, they moved to the Hotel Lenox for three nights so that the Dayers would have enough room for Cindy's bridesmaids, all of whom were from out of town.

DOROTHY (Diary)

1988

July 30: We came over [to the Dayers] for pictures and to see the bride come down the stairs and she was breathtakingly lovely. . . The wedding ceremony was simply beautiful. Three ministers officiated---one of them, Tim Kennedy, Cindy's cousin; also, a Catholic Priest and Rev. Dean Richardson---an old family friend. Larry took Bobbi down the aisle and young Roger took me and I walked with only my cane. . . .the Reception and dinner were just wonderful in every way…We left about 11 after the bride threw her bouquet and Iris [young Roger's fiancée] caught it!

Aug. 5: I met Iris, Bea and Wilma [friends from Suburban Women's Club] for lunch and then we played bridge in Wilma's lovely air-conditioned home. We spoke of the fact that we've played together for 15 summers and I'm sure the thought that it might be our last time was in all our minds.

Aug. 25: [Villa Serena] The day we came home we heard of the death of our dear friend of many years, Clifford Allen. He was 87 and had suffered from Bone Cancer for several years.

Sept. 6: We had a real treat in the form of a visit from our friends of almost 60 years---Ray and Treva Grimes. We were friends in our early married days but they moved to Vallejo, CA over 40 years ago but we've always kept in touch and have seen each other occasionally.

Sept. 12: The Seniorcize Class began again and we both went. I'm going to <u>try</u> to go to that regularly.

EDITOR

Phyllis Rogers' wedding, October 11, 1988, provided the occasion for another happy Allbert family get-together. Cindy Dayer Erb was one of her cousin's attendants.

DOROTHY: (Diary)

Oct. 1: The wedding was at 3 in the Menlo Park Presbyterian Church and it was a truly memorable ceremony... The reception was at the Burlingame Country Club in a beautiful, enormous clubhouse, which was a former mansion... There were over 250 guests... Roy made a beautiful speech and introduced family members. All 4 of the Bride's grandparents were present which I'm sure is a bit unusual...

Oct. 25: The Villa Halloween party...For the second-time Gene won the prize for the best costume.

EDITOR

Hardly had the Allberts recovered from granddaughter Phyllis's wedding when it was time to leave for granddaughter Katie Clarke's wedding on Long Island, NY. Gene and Dorothy flew with Ruth and Roy and experienced flying first class for the first time.

DOROTHY: (Diary)

Oct. 27: We had first class tickets and it was <u>so</u> elegant--- wonderful food, a free movie, free drinks, roomy seats---I really like it!

Oct. 28: At the Rehearsal Dinner, "They had a cake to celebrate Gene's 80th birthday . . .

Oct. 29: Katie's wedding day dawned bright and clear though not very warm . . . The wedding was in a beautiful old Catholic church . . . the reception was at the Bethpage Country Club . . . There was much dancing and the Bride & Groom just had such a happy time dancing and mingling with their family and guests.

Oct. 30: Peggy drove Ruth, Gene and me to the Air Port & we had a lovely flight home with a delicious dinner . . . It is such a relief to be back in this quite peaceful place again . . . I'm glad the weddings are all over.

EDITOR

By the end of November, the Allberts were traveling again - - - this time to their daughter Peggy's home, to celebrate Thanksgiving.

DOROTHY: (Diary)

<u>1988</u>

Nov. 22: Ruth came and drove us to the Air Port. It is a very pleasant flight to Denver and only about 2 ½ hours but we lose an hour because of the change to Mountain time. Thanksgiving Day was beautiful. We watched Macy's parade and had a delicious Turkey dinner about 4. Mary Ellen and George and Thomas came as well as John III, Mark and Stephanie so there were 10 of us...

Dec. 28: For more than two weeks I busily wrote Christmas cards and letters and Gene did a few also and we sent out over 60 Christmas greetings and received more than that. On the 18th we went in to see Ruth and Roy a while to say "goodbye" as they left for Hawaii on Monday the 19th... We came on to the Rogers' house to spend the night as we will be doing for the next 18 nights while they are in Hawaii. Christmas Eve Morning we met Cindy and Steve at the San Jose Airport and brought them back to Rogers and we have had a delightful day together. I'm so glad I planned good meals to eat here as the weather has been just terrible... We ate Christmas dinner at the Villa.

EDITOR

In the election of 1980, the Democratic candidate, President Jimmy Carter, had been defeated by Republican candidate, Ronald Reagan, previously known to the American people as a movie star. President Carter had been unable to solve the Iranian hostage crisis, in which more than 60 American diplomats and citizens had been held captive for 444 days. A few hours after Reagan's inauguration, the captives were released.

      During the Reagan era (1981-1989), the American public was encouraged to once again take pride in their country after the dramatic social rebellions and upheavals of the 60's and 70's. The 1980's were a time of social calm and widespread prosperity. In the election of 1988, Vice President George H. W. Bush easily defeated his Democratic rival, George Dukakis, so the Republicans continued in office for four more years until Democrat Bill Clinton defeated President Bush in 1992.

DOROTHY: (Diary)

<u>1989</u>

Jan. 18: Authors' Party for some people in a writing class. They had all written a short story of Memoirs and a book called "Glimpses" was made from them and Gene had written one of the stories ["Our Kitchen Stove"] so he was one of the honored authors.

Jan. 20: Inauguration Day and seeing it all on TV has been very interesting. It seems as though President Bush and his white-haired matronly wife Barbara are great people and I hope their term in the White House will be a good one for them and our country.

Jan. 25: Gene went to the Monte Carlo night and won a beautiful pot of crocuses which are in full bloom. <u>He</u>, who doesn't believe in gambling---even thinks it is sinful---always goes to the Monte Carlo night, plays Roulette and usually wins a prize. Amusing!

Feb. 4: Gene never misses anything. On Wednesday, he packed some grocery bags at the church, then went to a Writers' class in the afternoon and right after supper went back to church to help with the Pioneer Club. He is just <u>too much</u>. Thursday, he had the Bible Study Class and the World Affairs Class and we were again asked to sit at the table with some prospective residents who were very interesting people. Friday the rain came at last and Gene bought some fluorescent lamps and put them over our cupboards and they light up our dark little kitchen so nicely. It seemed good to have him at home.

EDITOR

The next grandchild's wedding was scheduled for August 12, 1989 in Buffalo. Roger E. Dayer married a college classmate, Iris Hanna. Dorothy had arranged to have knee replacement surgery in Buffalo after the wedding so that she could recuperate at the Dayers.

DOROTHY: (Diary)

<u>1989</u>

July 30: We got to Buffalo about 7:30 and both Bobbi and Dr. were there to meet us. It is so pleasant to be here again.

Aug. 1: Dr. Sterman [the orthopedic surgeon] has scheduled the joint replacement operation for Aug. 16. I dread it but it seems I'll soon be in a wheel chair unless I have it done. We'll probably be here until Oct. 1.

Aug. 12: The wedding [at Central Park United Methodist Church] was beautiful. I came home and rested after the wedding so missed the reception, which everyone said was lovely, too. However, the Open House here in the evening was lovely---only about 20 people here and the meal was catered. They surprised me with a birthday cake and a beautiful Mother's ring from my 3 daughters. I'm so blessed by having them.

Aug. 16: . . . my knee joint replacement is to be this afternoon.

Sept. 19: It will be five weeks tomorrow since I last wrote in here. I went in the hospital and had my knee joint replacement as scheduled. It seems kind of hazy to me now. . . I was in the hospital 12 days and then came "home" to Bobbi and Roger's house. Everyone was so good to me . . . I've had close to a hundred "get well" cards . . . Gene has been wonderful as always through all this. He had to give me quite a lot of care when I first came home . . . [The Dayers both were working full time.]

EDITOR

Dorothy had many visitors while she recuperated. Due to her inability to climb the stairs, she stayed in the 1st floor den where there was an adjoining bathroom. The ever-resourceful Gene expanded a built-in leather couch with plywood and brought down a mattress from the second floor to create a bed for Dorothy.

DOROTHY: (Diary)

Sept. 25: . . . the big event of the day is that I climbed all the stairs to the 2nd floor!

Oct. 9: We are back home in Calif... Everyone here seems glad to have us back and so many have said so.

Nov. 7: Life is so much pleasanter without pain!

Nov. 21: I have Macular Degeneration, which is quite resistant to treatment. Dr. Whitney said it won't cause complete blindness but even now I have difficulty reading.

Dec. 8: I have <u>all</u> the Christmas cards addressed and about half of them with letters or notes written and in the mail.

Dec. 18: One Christmas card brought the sad news that Mildred Canfield died last April. We had known each other since I was 3 and she was 6.

Pam [the activities director] was here a while this morning and wants me to do some writing for the "News & Views". It should be interesting if my eyesight just holds out. I try not to worry about the Macular Degeneration but can't help being aware of it.

Dec. 20: I made the Fantastic Fudge on Wednesday, with Gene's help and have shared it with several people.

Dec. 25: Christmas Day was very quiet and somewhat lonely for us as we were all alone for the first time in many years, but we had wonderful talks with all three of our precious daughters; many presents to open and a delicious dinner here at the Villa. [All the Rogers were in Hawaii and the Erbs in Buffalo].

1990

March 11: We were invited with Ruth and Roy to their friends the Robinsons in Santa Cruz and we had a lovely time. Marieta Robinson is a wonderful cook and she and Norman are very much our kind of people ... They are simple, unsophisticated people like we are.

March 28: Cindy [Erb] and Phyllis [Bedford] both pregnant.

April 4: On Thursday, the 29th of March, I got my new reading glasses and also a special lamp which puts all the light right on the reading material. It is still difficult but I can manage the newspaper and Readers Digest now ...

April 30: We are all looking forward to our 60th Anniversary celebration and family reunion in just two months.

May 24: Things here at the Villa continue very pleasantly for us but some people have a hard time. One dear old lady who has been here about 3 months just couldn't find a regular place to eat---people wouldn't let her sit at their table, so finally I asked to have a larger table set up for us and a place for her so now there are 5 at our table and she is so pleased.

EDITOR

Since Cindy was expecting her first child in June, she knew she could not be at the 60th Anniversary Celebration, so she invited her grandparents to come to San Diego, to see the Erbs' new house. Dorothy wrote an account of the visit on June 20th.

DOROTHY: (Diary)

June 1: Cindy met us and took us home for lunch on their patio and in the evening, she had a special dinner to celebrate our coming 60th anniversary...She had a special ice cream cake and gave us a lovely album... Saturday the 2nd we drove around the rich suburb of La Jolla... Sunday the 3rd we drove to Coronado Beach and saw the beautiful beach and Hotel Coronado. Luxurious..

June 12: It is a dear little girl named Natalie Dayer Erb.

June 20: Gene is as hyper active as ever---constantly busy at something. He has recently made two wind chimes... and was paid for them.

EUGENE: 'Things I have Made" (Essay, written in 2000)

After we moved to Santa Clara I became interested in making wind chimes. Some of the excess copper sheet from Roy Roger's roof could be used to make ornaments for the wind chimes, I thought. I made an outline of a rooster and a pelican and cut out four or five of each from the copper. Each chime had five to seven pipes, cut from ½ inch steel conduit, aluminum or copper pipe. These each were made differently and either given away or sold. The one I am keeping is made with ten pipes of three different metals and does not have an ornament. The chime was held up from a hole in the top of the ornament's head and the chime held to the bottom of the feet. The poles were of different lengths to provide the different tones when struck. These were made in the mid-1990s.

EDITOR

The Allberts' apartment at the Villa Serena had a small outdoor patio where the wind chimes were hung. They could be heard in the living room through the French doors, as well as on the patio. Gene also liked to make walking sticks for people from interesting wood branches he collected on beaches and other places. These carved walking sticks really were works of art; both beautiful and useful.

The next big event was the 60th anniversary celebration, which was a thrilling occasion for the Allbert family.

DOROTHY: (Diary)

June 22: This will probably be the last time I write in this journal until after July 1st. Great plans are being made by our 3 daughters to celebrate our 60th wedding anniversary here at the Villa on June 30th. Our 3 girls and their husbands will be here, all of our grandchildren except dear little Cindy and her baby...

I have a beautiful ring which Gene bought me two weeks ago as an anniversary gift. I picked it out myself and I like it very much. It is a pear shaped purple sapphire with small diamonds on each side. It looks nice on my hand.

July 11: It is almost three weeks since I wrote in here last and what a happy time it has been. Our Anniversary celebration began on June 24th [with the arrival of the first group of children and grandchildren.]

July 13: To continue the account of our Anniversary celebration: About 5:00 11 of us left here in 3 cars- - - ours, Vernon's and Clarkes rented cars and drove into Rogers where we were confronted with a large sign proclaiming our 60th Anniversary. There was some picture taking and then a really jolly family party. There were 21 of us; 8 of our grandchildren and 2 of their mates. How we would have loved to have Cindy and Stephen and darling Natalie there but she was just too new to make the trip. The weather was perfect and some of the crowd went in the pool and there was a delicious Lasagna dinner---buffet style. Ruth managed it all so well and I'm sure it was enjoyed by all.

July 17: I'll continue with the saga of our celebration. The Anniversary this year came on Saturday, which made it perfect for our reception in the afternoon...

Phyllis [Rogers Bedford] and Katie [Clarke Sommers] arrived with a beautiful corsage for me, and a boutonnière for Gene---gifts from the grandchildren. When we got out into the garden the band was playing and many, many people from the Villa and family members, too, were there ... over 100 in all. It was all just lovely- - -the sign was hung out by the pond- - -there were pink and white balloons flying and beautifully decorated tables and everything was so festive....

After a little while to rest during which there was a small earthquake to show the non-Californians what they are like, we all gathered again at a nice restaurant---Pacific Seafood---in Sunnyvale for a lovely dinner for 27 of us--- all family except Ruth and Don Dell [friends of Peggy's] ..

.There just aren't any words to tell how happy this time has been for us or how much we appreciate our daughters, their husbands and the grandchildren and now the precious great-grandchildren. ... .

What a "Mountain Top" experience it has been! I am so grateful for all the good things God has done for us.

Aug. 10: Cindy, Steve and precious baby Natalie visited us last week-end . . . the baby is just beautiful and unbelievably good.

Aug. 21: There is a serious International Crisis just now in the Persian Gulf and it could mean a war but I hope and pray not!

EDITOR

The Persian Gulf Crisis began when the Iraqis invaded Kuwait and President Bush sent American troops to defend Kuwait as part of a United Nations coalition. Fortunately, the war ended quickly and the Kuwaiti government was restored in March, 1991.

Current events were discussed as part of the Santa Clara Senior Citizen Program classes held at the Villa Serena,

DOROTHY: (Diary)

1990

Sept. 27: The classes here have resumed and Gene is happy and busy with several of them and I have started to take a class in Conversational Spanish. Usually I don't like classes and I very much dislike Study and Discussion groups, but this promises to be interesting as I had several years of Spanish in my long ago school days.

Oct. 18: Gene's 82nd birthday. One of the cards from a resident here is a perfect description of Gene---"strength of iron, nerves of steel and a heart of gold".

Nov. 3: Politics are the Prime subject of discussion. Gene has been very active here at the Villa in getting Absentee ballots for people and helping them vote... I hate politics, personally, but guess they are a necessary evil. I think most politicians are highly paid crooks.

Halloween, the 31st day of October, 1990, will always be a special one in our family because at about 9:15 p.m., Sarah Elizabeth Bedford was born.

Dec. 20: It has been over 3 weeks since I last wrote in here and it has been a very busy and mostly happy time... Nov. 27: Cindy and precious Natalie arrived. On the 28th we went in to the Rogers and Phyllis was there with precious 5 week old Sarah and the two cousins had such a good time with their babies... It was such a joy to be together... Dec. 5: Larry [Dayer, Roger and Roberta's oldest son] came to pay us a visit and we had a lovely time with him too... The great annual job of getting the Christmas cards and letters done has been accomplished... I'm afraid by next year my eyes will be too bad to get out the cards.

EDITOR

Dorothy and Gene flew to Denver to celebrate Christmas with Peggy's family.

DOROTHY: (Diary)

Dec. 22: On Thursday the 13th we went to Benjamin Bubb school where Ruth directs the Musical Education Program and heard the children give their Christmas program. It was very nice really and we enjoyed it. It had been a long time since we had been to a school program. Then Ruth took us to lunch at a nice Italian Restaurant and I had Spumoni ice cream---a very special treat to me.

Now we have been in Denver 2 days and I haven't been out of the house. The weather is just unbelievably cold---0 [degrees] for nearly 48 hours and will continue... Stephanie is to arrive tonight.

1991

Jan. 1: New Year's Day, 1991! In the ten days since I last wrote a lot has happened. Peggy had tickets for us all to go to a dinner Theatre and see Camelot-a stage play. We met Mark, his fiancé, Rachel, and her 10-year-old son Chris at the theatre. The dinner and play were both excellent... Christmas Eve: 12 of us had a delicious Turkey and all the trimmings dinner... It was all as pleasant as it could possibly have been... Cindy, Steve and Natalie were at Dayers'.

EDITOR

While Gene and Dorothy were in Denver, John Clarke's sister Phyllis, who lived in Boston, had a stroke.

Peg and John flew to Boston and brought her back to Denver to stay in a nearby nursing home, since Phyllis had no other relatives to care for her. Gene and Dorothy stayed with Stephie and took care of the house until Peggy returned with Phyllis. John stayed in Boston "to conclude Phyllis's financial affairs."

DOROTHY (Diary)

Jan. 18: The time in Denver was pleasant all the way through and we got a number of things done with Peggy. She is just such a fine person and I love her more all the time... Jan. 17 will go down in history as the day war between the U.S. and Iraq was finally declared. ...We don't dare think of what the future may bring but must keep our faith. I feel so sorry for people who do not trust and believe in the Lord....

This will probably be my last journal entry. It is getting increasingly hard to write- - - my eyes are deteriorating and life goes on so quietly most of the time it is hardly worth recording.

Jan. 29: Must add a few final lines to tell of the birth of Valerie Rose Ward on Jan. 24th... I'm so glad Mary Ellen [Clarke Ward] has a daughter.

EDITOR

Fortunately, shortly before Dorothy stopped writing in her diaries and sending the Christmas cards, Eugene began writing his autobiography and also wrote an annual Christmas letter, so the firsthand account of their lives at the Villa continued. Dorothy served as Gene's consultant on dates, spelling and interpretation.

When the Allberts moved to California in 1987, they had stored some of their things on the 3rd floor at the Dayers' house, including Dorothy's diaries. Roberta brought the diaries to California a few at a time, so that her parents could consult them in writing their autobiographies. However, since she was a historian, Roberta was conscious of the diaries' irreplaceability, so she insisted on taking them back to Buffalo to prevent them from being lost.

GENE: (Autobiography)

     Mark [Clarke] and Rachel had announced plans to be married on June 29, 1991. Dorothy and I went to Buffalo earlier so we could attend the wedding in Denver on our way home. Our visit with Bobbi and Roger was one of the most pleasant we have had. Dorothy was well and Bobbi had two big parties for us: one with some of the Camera Club members, and one with a general group of friends.

     Margaret had reserved rooms at the Hilton Hotel in Denver for all of us to stay. . . I think we all had a good time. Probably the fellowship and visiting were more memorable to most of us than the wedding itself.

     Vernon [Gene's brother] had driven to Denver and he and I went to Raton: down on one day, visited, and returned the next. While there we went to the Fairmont Cemetery and visited our parents' graves and I made a rubbing of the stone markers. Dad's first wife's name was Scena I. and dates 1875-1902. Mother's name was Louise K., and dates 1874-1965. Dad's name, Alva W. dates 1874-1954... We then went to Gardiner. We walked up the canyon until I became too tired and came back to the car. There were only two buildings standing in Gardiner, the area did not show it had ever existed as a town. We spread the weeds apart and found the stones that were once a part of the foundation of our house. There were bare places that were once a road.

EDITOR

The weddings of grandchildren and births of great grandchildren continued throughout the 90s. Fortunately, Gene created a family tree, which is helpful in keeping track of the growing family. Gene continued to take on new responsibilities while Dorothy's health deteriorated further. They were able to make three more trips to Buffalo in the early 90s, but after Stephie Clarke's wedding in Rochester, NY in 1994, Dorothy announced that henceforth, her family would have to come to her in California. And come they did!

GENE: (Autobiography)

In early 1992, Dorothy's sight had become so poor that her doctor declared her legally blind. She now was able to receive the "Talking Books" and the tape playing machine.

We went to Buffalo again in August,'92 and enjoyed having friends at the Dayers' for visits. Vernon came while we were there and we finished the flagstone walk that we had worked on the previous year. Daniel

Eugene Erb was born October 5, 1992---our third great-grandson. Bobbi planned another Christmas at La Jolla and we had our tickets to go. Dorothy broke her hip on December 18 and was taken to El Camino Hospital. They operated and added a steel plate and screws to hold it in place. Peggy came the next day and stayed several days. Bobbi was here for a couple of days before Christmas. The Rogers, who had flown to Hawaii the day before Dorothy broke her hip, kept in touch by phone. Peggy came again to help Dorothy when she came home.

I started volunteering in the Intergenerational Program at Briarwood School in the 1992-93 year. We were working with first grade students in Mrs. Karen Kanani's room.

EDITOR

Gene's granddaughter, Cindy, gave him a computer and printer which proved to be of great help in his writing. She taught him how to use it and one of the other residents at the Villa provided day-to-day assistance. Eugene continued to report the births of the great-grandchildren.

EUGENE: (Autobiography)

Rebecca Bedford was born on March 26, 1993. She is the second daughter of Phyllis and Scott and another great granddaughter for us. Roger E. and Iris Dayer had twin daughters on June 15, 1993. Their names are Brianna Claire and Kyla Nicole, ninth and tenth great grandchildren for us.

We went to Buffalo in August again, this time by Air Canada and Bobbi and Roger met us in Toronto. Roger E. and Iris brought the twins from Croton-on-Hudson to see us. The Sommers family, Katie and Kelly; Vernon and Stephanie were all there for a visit. Dorothy was less able to get around and her friends came to Dayers' to see her.

Robert William Sommers was born on February 12, 1994 to Kathleen and Robert. Our family continues to expand. I went to see the Erb family the weekend of May 20, 1994. Roberta and Vernon visited us on June 9, 1994. They were here to attend the wedding of David [Rogers] and Laura [Park] who were married on June 11.

We went to Buffalo the middle of September, 1994. Stephanie Clarke and Jeff Booth were to be married the eighth of October, 1994 and we wanted to do some visiting before that date. Margaret had made reservations at the Hotel Strathallan in Rochester for our headquarters for the wedding. Many of our family were there... Mary Ellen and Katie were the Bridesmaids. The wedding was held in an Episcopal Church with a woman priest officiating. I enjoyed her instructions to the couple and the ceremony. Jeffrey Booth had many members of his family and friends in attendance. David and Laura announced at the reception that they were expecting a baby in June 1995. Conrad David Rogers was born on June 4, 1995.

The year 1995 had some very happy events... My autobiography was progressing well; the first part that Margaret had typed was on a disc. I had it copied on paper so that I could edit it. The computer that Cindy gave me permitted me to type the years 1960 on from records, memory and Dorothy's recollection. Cindy came up in March and brought a printer to use with the computer.

The 65th wedding anniversary was celebrated with a dinner at Ruth and Roy's on June 30, 1995 and another dinner at Marianni's Motel on July 1, where many of the family stayed. Most of the extended family attended. We felt well honored. Sunday the 2nd we enjoyed brunch at the Villa. The children played on the lanai and watched the ducks. The Villa management gave me a plaque with my picture on it, naming the library, "The Eugene F. Allbert Library". Our children were here to see the plaque mounted on the wall.

EDITOR

As part of the 65th Wedding Anniversary celebration, the grandchildren wrote letters to Nana and Boppa, describing their influence in their lives. I quote a few excerpts:

Mary Ellen Clarke Ward, who had made a quilt for them:

"As I was sewing, I came to realize more clearly that many times, in our society, we miss the Process. Our lives are a collection of pieces. They may be beautiful, good, bad, or boring, but they all fit together. What differentiates our "quilts" is how we sew them together (the process or our morals) Do we live each day with love and care? Take care of each other? Are we kind to a stranger? Thank you for teaching and showing me the right way to sew my quilt."

Mark Clarke: "Nana and Boppa, I will always remember your patience, competence and love of life. . .. As you understand, losing my brother was a great shock. During that time of great tragedy, I drew strength and renewed faith from all that I have learned from you. I understood that John's pain was ended, and that he went to a better place."

Katie Clarke Sommers: "Nana, I always remember walking into your beautiful home as a child. You always took such pride in your home, something we both share. I'm always amazed at how incredible your memory is and what a great sense of humor you have."

Phyllis Rogers Bedford: "I know times were not always easy for you when you were raising your children. However, what is so evident in your three girls is that they received a lot of love and moral guidance. . . Both of you continue to be solid role models for your children, grandchildren and now great grandchildren."

Cynthia Dayer Erb quotes from a book by Judith Wallerstein, "as your influence on my life has truly shaped my values, and marriage particularly: 'good marriages need to be part of our legacy to future generations. A good marriage is more than the happy possession of an individual couple and their children. It is this unit.. .that shapes adults and children. More than any other human institution, marriage is the vehicle for transmitting our values to future generations.'

GENE: (Autobiography)

On my 87th birthday [October 18, 1995] I received many cards and telephone calls. This getting older is not so bad after all. I was honored as "Student of the Year" at an Open House held at the Senior Center by the Santa Clara Unified School District's Education Options Department. I was given a plaque for my records.

The year 1996 started with the usual program of volunteering in the fourth grade and in the Intergenerational program for the first grade. The writing class at the Villa was interesting and I enjoyed preparing a typed page for each assignment. Thomas Samuel Erb was born on February 19, 1996.

In May, [1996] Margaret received her BA degree in journalism. Dorothy would not be able to attend the graduation exercises but I wanted to be there. I flew to Denver on May 9 and had an enjoyable week with the family. Margaret won a scholarship for a ten-day course in journalism at the University of Florida in a national contest.

EDITOR

Since the Erbs lived in San Diego, which was only an hour away by plane, they were able to see Boppa quite often. Thus, Gene became well acquainted with Natalie and Danny.

GENE: (Autobiography)

The Erb family brought Thomas Samuel, who was born February 19th, to see us in June. I made plans to visit the Erb family on the 25th to 27th of October. It was a very good visit. We made plans for a workbench for Erbs' garage area. Steve and Danny built it during the next two weeks.

EDITOR

During the latter half of the decade, Gene and Dorothy's life became quieter as one would expect with people in their late 80s. Their children and grandchildren continued to visit them frequently which they of course enjoyed, but Dorothy gradually grew weaker. Late in 1997, Gene reported: "Dorothy and I are slowing down. Time is catching up with us." When the time came to plan Gene's 90th birthday celebration, the daughters decided on a quiet family dinner at the Los Altos Country Club. On October 18, 1998, thirteen family members were present. To mark the occasion, Margaret gave a gift to the Denver Seminary to create "The Eugene Allbert Award" which would assist a student with financial need for his or her tuition expenses. The Dayer grandchildren wrote Boppa letters, full of memories, excerpts of which follow:

CINDY: Happy Birthday! 90 years! I have so many memories of our times together growing up in Buffalo: Christmas Eve dinners and slide shows with all the trimmings; your red Christmas vest; New Year's Eve with chips and dip. Saturday mornings when you would come to 143 [Woodbridge] to fix whatever was broken. Sunday lunch after church, camera always in hand; expressions such as "For the love of Pete"; peanut butter and pickle sandwiches; cranberry sauce; our drive to the

University of Michigan when the big red car broke down; your visit to New York City to see where I was working and living...and now I get to see a part of you all over again so evident in my children.

Boppa, I love you very much---you and Nana have always been a second set of parents to me and I can never truly thank you for all the guidance and direction you have given me. When things seem tough I always try to think about what you and Nana would do...just hang in and keep going forward! Thank you for writing your autobiography, which our children will continue to read and ask questions about for years to come.

ROGER E.: Boppa, you have influenced me in so many ways I don't know where to begin. Some of my fondest childhood memories were all the times I spent with you and Nana. Whether we were playing '99', bowling, fishing or just talking, I always had a great time. You never lectured me about how I should live my life but you were always setting a wonderful example for me to try to emulate. Although you were always working you still made time to help so many others. The volunteer work you did delivering food to the poor and also all the work at Camp Vick (Don't you ever get tired?) especially taught me the value of giving to others.

LARRY: I have so many early memories of Boppa that it is difficult to decide where to start. I was very fortunate because I was the oldest in my family and resided in the same city, so I had a virtual monopoly on the attentions of three doting grandparents. I even got to meet "Big Momma" [Louise Allbert}...

Our fishing expeditions are probably my favorite memories. When I was probably 11 or 12, I have a very clear memory of Boppa and I in the canoe in the middle of the lake at Camp Vick. I think we had brought along my friend Steve also. It was a warm June day and we had all just pulled in a few bass and Boppa said: "Now why would someone want to be chasing around a little white ball when they could be doing this?"

EDITOR

Unfortunately, Dorothy's health continued to grow worse in the late 90s, first with the diagnosis of Diabetes, and then with an eye infection leading to total blindness in one eye. But the presence and assistance of Ruth's family, and the frequent visits of children, grandchildren and great-grandchildren, enabled Gene and Dorothy to cope with their problems and to continue enjoying life at the Villa Serena as the century drew to a close.

GENE: (Autobiography)

The first of the year 2000 and the new millennium came in as so many others have. The Y2K scare caused many businesses, universities, and airlines to review their computer programs and correct any errors they found. Margaret went home the first of January after a very pleasant visit with many of her California relations. All of the regular events were back on schedule. Dorothy's left eye has drops two times a day. She has no sight in that eye.

Stephanie brought Jackson [born June 14, 1999] to see us on March 10. She stayed at Ruth's because Ruth had the equipment for baby care. Jackson made quite a hit. I found he would smile and laugh when I whistled. He is a grand baby. Dorothy said not to leave him alone because someone would steal him.

EDITOR

In May of 2000, Dorothy fell again, this time breaking her pelvis. In order to recover, she would be required to lie flat on her back for six weeks.

GENE: (Autobiography)

May 18: Dorothy was transferred to the Grant-Cuesta Rehab. Center and seems in good spirits. Bobbi arrived for a few days; Ruth and Gene visited every day and Peggy came in June.

June 30: Our 70th wedding anniversary was celebrated at the Grant-Cuesta Nursing and Rehabilitation Center. The management there made the plans to have it in their inner court. All went well and we had a happy time. The Center Management, many of the residents in their wheel chairs, the staff, and representatives from other groups were there. Ruth and Roy, Roberta and Roger, Phyllis and Rebecca, and David, Laura and their three, and I attended. It was a happy party.

August 13: Bobbi arrived yesterday and Ruth and Bobbi planned a dinner for Dorothy's 90th birthday at the Center to be held in the inner court. Roy, Ruth and I moved tables together and placed fancy tablecloths on them. . . Ruth and Roy brought the food and the cake. Phyllis, Scott, and their two, [Sarah and Rebecca] David

Laura, and their three, [Conrad, Roxanne and Trevor] Ruth, Roy, Bobbi, Dorothy and I enjoyed a good meal of ribs, chicken, baked beans, muffins and cabbage salad. It was a very happy occasion. Tomorrow is Dorothy's birthday.

EDITOR

While Dorothy was in the Nursing Home, she and Gene received a long letter from Bobbi Robinson Lawson (the girls' childhood friend) who regularly corresponded with them. Some years after Gene's death in 2009, Bobby sent the letter to the Editor. It was dated August 20, 2000. After Bobbi R (Robinson) lost her mother, she sometimes confided her troubles to Gene and Dorothy. Dorothy dictated the first part of the letter to Gene in the Nursing Home. This letter may have been Dorothy's final written words. The second part, by Gene, beautifully conveys Gene's philosophy of life. Dorothy and Bobby "R" both had August birthdays.

DOROTHY to Bobby R: On August 14, 2000, my birthday, the doctor said my fractures had healed and I could learn to get around again. It has been over three months since I left the Villa so I'm ready to go back. Best birthday wishes, Mrs. "A".

GENE to Bobby R: Now it is my turn: I wanted to write to you but Dorothy wanted to dictate her own letter and now she has done it. I am doing all right with all of the support Ruth and her children give. They visit often except Ruth is there every day. Bobbi and Peggy call every evening and I make three calls a day and a visit every day. I think she is getting spoiled, don't you?

I hope you are able to solve most of your problems. The thing I try to do is, I say to myself "I'll live through it and still have some love for those whom I serve." This is sometimes hard to do, but we must keep our health and realize there are others who can help. It might cost money but you have to be alive to help at all. Chin up, don't let it get you down.

GENE: (Autobiography)

Sept. 1, 2000: About 11:30 p.m., I awoke with a sore shoulder. I rubbed it but it didn't go away. I dressed because it seemed serious. Around 1:00 a.m., the 2nd, I pressed the emergency button and soon Edith, our Co-Manager, was at the door. . . the ambulance took me to the emergency room at El Camino Hospital. . . The continued testing indicated I had a heart attack and that a vein on the heart was blocked. Dr. Masters, a cardiologist, ran a treadmill test on me and said it could be possible to do more testing, but at my age we should try medications. Dr. Gilman [the internist] agreed and I came home with more prescriptions on the 5th.

Sept. 7: Dorothy came home. . . We have a nurse helping. Her name is Alem and she is here to get Dorothy ready for the day and comes again at night and puts her to bed.

Oct. 24: Dorothy was getting dressed with Alem's [a Nurse's Aid] help the morning of October 24. She felt her left leg go limp and soon she was in the El Camino Hospital again. She was diagnosed with poor circulation in that leg and the blockage was some place above her hip. She suffered with this and was given morphine to limit the pain. By the 26th she was incoherent part of the time and on the 28th was asleep when we visited her. Dorothy passed away at 5:30 p.m. on October 28, 2000.

EDITOR

Dorothy had written her own Memorial Service in advance and even had Roberta practice reading the specified Bible passage! In addition, Dorothy and Gene had taken each of their daughters to the cemetery to see the gravesite where their Memorial Stone would be placed. Naturally all three daughters came to the Villa when their mother died. Plans were made for Eugene to come to Buffalo to be with the Dayers for the Christmas holidays.

GENE: (Autobiography)

Margaret arrived from Denver the morning of the 28th. She made phone calls on the 29th and took charge of contacting the Memorial Park and the Hospital. Sunday, we made the arrangements for the Memorial Service. Joe Howard offered to play the organ and Maxine Cintas said she would take care of the refreshments to be available after the service. . . .

Nov. 1: The service was wonderful, just like Dorothy had planned. Pastor Bob gave a short review of Dorothy's illnesses and of her faith . . .about 100 persons attended . . . The whole event could not have gone better. I was very thankful for our daughters' effective handling of all the details.

EDITOR

In November, rather than sending the usual Christmas letter to their many friends and family members, Gene sent a Memorial letter:

GENE:

As many of you know, Dorothy, my beloved wife of 70 years, passed away peacefully at El Camino Hospital on 28 October 2000, after choosing not to have surgery for an embolism. After breaking her pelvis, the previous May, Dorothy had made a valiant effort to recover and had returned to the Villa Serena in September. However, as she grew weaker, the quality of her life declined until she no longer wished to live. I, and my daughters, are very grateful that Dorothy and I were able to celebrate our 70th anniversary in June and her 90th birthday in August.

We thought this letter should be one of Thanksgiving for all the blessings of friendship and love, which our family has enjoyed over these many years. All three of my daughters were with me for the Memorial Service, as were two sons-in-law, six grandchildren and five great grandchildren. Our friends from the church and the Villa and my school associates all shared in the celebration of Dorothy's warm and giving spirit.

EDITOR

And so ended, a 70-year love story.

Conclusion

Gene and Dorothy: A 70 Year Love Story

Gene and Dorothy's marriage was not an example of romantic love, where two young people fall in love and live happily ever after. For Gene, it was: But not for Dorothy. Gene often said that he knew he wanted to marry Dorothy the first time he saw her, when she was only five years old! I also believe that he never stopped being "in love" with my mother; continuing to view her through "rose-colored glasses". All their lives together, he drove her crazy taking photos of her!

For Dorothy, the situation was quite different. Even though Gene had been her high school sweetheart. I think her decision to marry him in 1930 came from a sense of desperation- - -she needed to escape from the threat of sexual abuse by her father. While we never discussed this, Dorothy's diary entries provide many suggestions to that effect. One blunt statement in her autobiography says that her father's attentions were not "strictly paternal."

But the first years of marriage were extremely difficult for Dorothy. She did not find it easy to live with Gene. It is clear that Gene's enormous energy; his devotion to his church, his thrift and refusal to indulge in any kind of luxury, strained their relationship many times over the years of their marriage. Dorothy was easy-going while Gene was a driver, never content to sit still. He was much more optimistic and naïve; she was fairly cynical.

They were very poor, with no family support and were forced to work extremely hard, with little time or money for relaxation during the first twenty-five years of their married life. But Dorothy always recognized that Gene was a good husband, completely loyal and devoted to her, despite the fact that she felt ignored much of the time. They shared the same values; both were deeply religious.

And they adored their three little girls, finding joy in raising them, in sacrificing for them. Gradually, over the long years, they learned to live happily together and to adapt to their differences. But it was not easy; it was an ongoing struggle! After they retired, things were much easier. They had enough money and traveling in the motor home made it possible for Dorothy to rest while Gene was out fishing. Living at the Villa Serena, Dorothy could pursue a quiet life without being alone. And Gene could move from class to class; project after project.

As Dorothy told Rich Kellman, the TV interviewer, at the time of their 50th anniversary: "There are ups and downs, good times and bad times." Fortunately, the bad times became fewer as they became more prosperous and as Dorothy developed an independent life. She gained confidence and received recognition and acknowledgment for her abilities and contributions. Her experiences as President of Suburban Women's Club provided the esteem and praise that she deserved.

For many years Gene and Dorothy felt socially inferior to many of their associates because neither of them had college degrees. It took many years before they realized how intellectually superior they were and how little a degree meant, when compared with a lifetime of education, which is what they possessed. In addition, their social life had suffered because they did not drink alcoholic beverages and did not know how to dance. But gradually they grew more confident.   As they watched their children gain advanced degrees, they began to realize how much they knew, despite the absence of a formal college education.

Eugene always had been more self-assured than Dorothy, but both were assertive people, good decision makers; natural leaders. Theirs always was a marriage of equals, in which Dorothy stood up for herself despite the ensuing emotional trauma.

And so, this seventy-year love story includes not the stuff of fairy tales, but the bricks and mortar necessary to build a happy marriage: self-discipline, hard work, dedication and commitment. What it lacks in romance, it gains in inspiration. For it proves the ability of two very different human beings to achieve that most difficult of all goals: a rewarding marriage.

Gene and Dorothy's legacy endures, continuing into the 21st century through their three daughters, nine grandchildren and seventeen great-grandchildren. In addition, people in three widely separated communities: Los Altos Hills, California; Denver, Colorado, and Buffalo, New York, continue to benefit from Allbert beliefs. In Los Altos Hills, Ruth Rogers dedicated a room at the New Performing Arts Center in their names.

In Denver, Margaret Clarke created a scholarship at the Denver Seminary to honor them; and in Buffalo, Roberta Dayer established the Dorothy and Eugene Allbert Fund for Women and Girls at the Community Foundation for Greater Buffalo. Is it any wonder that they died contented?

Epilogue

Gene and Dorothy

Living without Dorothy, 2001-2009

EDITOR

Gene must have been very lonely following Dorothy's death but characteristically, he did not complain. Rather, he continued his usual routine at the Villa- - - up at 6:30; Bible reading; breakfast at 8:00 a.m.; dinner at noon; supper at 5:30 p.m.; a nap after dinner and participation in the various daily classes, bus trips etc. He continued to work on his computer, writing both his autobiography and various essays for the Writing Class and Current Events Class.

His last letter to Al Robinson, described his new walker: "I am still getting along quite well. I use a walker to steady myself when I walk around the Villa and when shopping. It has four six inch wheels, brakes, a basket, and a seat that I use when I'm waiting in a line. It folds up so I can put it in the car." (dated March 8, 2002, and sent to Roberta Dayer by Bobbi Robinson Lawson, with the note that 'Al died the next month'.)

The Santa Clara Adult Education Program published a Newsletter in 2006-7, which included Gene's essay, "Talking Can Stop Hate". This may have been his last published work.

Gene wrote:

> "We in our own way each day will find talking a pleasant time if we're not trying to force others to adopt our ideas. When we respect others' backgrounds and they understand and respect ours, a good conversation can be held and both parties will be enhanced."

As Gene became acquainted with people of different nationalities and traditions, he gradually grew more liberal, accepting those with different backgrounds and beliefs.

Other responsibilities included taking the photos of newcomers; arranging the monthly birthday photo display for the dining room and volunteering at the local elementary school until 2005, when he stopped driving. Every Sunday Gene attended the morning Bible Class; then greeted those arriving for Church, seated on his walker, where the school children gave him hugs. He continued serving as a greeter until two weeks before he died.

After Gene received a "Humanitarian Award" in 1999 from the Villa Serena Management, one of his residents, Gladys Zacharisen, wrote an essay describing Gene's activities, an excerpt of which follows:

> "On a sunny day you just might see him caring for the rose bushes along the driveway. He helps people in wheelchairs, get where they need to go. He opens doors for them to get in and out. He stops and talks to

people when they ask him questions; with that lovely smile, he always has on his face. I

would like to say thank you Gene, thank you for all the time you give us willingly and never let down that beautiful smile of yours. Not too many people these days are like you." (March 30, 1999)

Gene remained very interested in the activities of his children and grandchildren. Having Ruth's family close by enabled him to enjoy all the major holidays with them except Christmas. The first Christmas after Dorothy died, Roberta came to accompany him to Buffalo where he spent a couple weeks. He went to the Brighton Baptist Church; the Westinghouse Retirees' luncheon and saw many former friends. In a later trip, he visited Cindy and Steve Erb in San Diego where he enjoyed teaching the great-grandchildren how to fish. Both Margaret and Roberta visited him several times a year. While Gene's physical strength gradually decreased throughout his 90s, his mind remained active and clear until he died.

Shortly before her death, while Dorothy was in the Nursing Home, she had talked with Gene about re-marrying after she died. She felt that he should not be alone. And so, in 2003, at age 95, Gene announced to his daughters that he and a fellow resident, Maggie Waldie, had decided to marry. Maggie, who was in her 80s, had been married twice before, but she still was pretty, active and fun to be with. Gene's daughters voiced no objections: Rather, they were pleased that their father had found a suitable companion for his final years.

The outdoor wedding took place at the Villa Serena in October 2003, with Ruth's family and Margaret attending and Maggie's son and daughter. (Roberta had been there the week before). Afterwards, the newlyweds drove down the coast of California to Monterey for a short honeymoon. Maggie gave up her apartment and moved in with Gene. Characteristically, Gene frankly described his motives in taking a second wife: He needed someone to take care of him! And Maggie was willing.

Since Maggie came from a much different background than Gene, the marriage required some adjustments. She was neither religious, nor philanthropic, nor did she have grandchildren. Thus the constant phone calls and visits of the Allbert family members came as a shock to her, as did Gene's commitment to his church and charities. Maggie was a fun-loving person who loved to dance and gamble. She frequently took weekend trips to Reno. Finally, Gene, to his daughters' amazement, accompanied Maggie on these gambling trips, despite the fact that he had adamantly opposed gambling all his life. And so, they both compromised and managed to live together fairly successfully for five years.

In October 2008, the couple celebrated Gene's 100th birthday and their 5th wedding anniversary at the Villa. All three daughters and two of their husbands, several Allbert grandchildren and a few great-grandchildren were there for the happy event, as well as Maggie's son and daughter. The next day Gene's three daughters, Roy Rogers and Dr. Dayer drove Maggie and

Gene back to Monterey to the hotel where they had spent their honeymoon. As they entered the hotel, one daughter carried the oxygen; one the walker and one the cane! Everything went smoothly and all enjoyed the celebration.

Sadly, in the months following his 100th birthday, it became clear that Gene's body finally was giving out. During the month of January, 2009, he had been taken to the emergency room by ambulance three times for heart failure. During the third hospitalization, Roberta and Maggie were with him in the hospital room when the Doctor and Nurse came in. The Doctor said: Mr. Allbert, here are your options: You can go to a nursing home (Gene sat up straight and said "never'), or you can have hospice care at home." Gene firmly responded: "I'll take hospice".

After the interview, Gene told Roberta: "I've had a wonderful life and I'm ready to go. I love people!" Maggie and Roberta took him home to the Villa the next day. Roberta read aloud the notes on his 40 Christmas cards with him and he reviewed all his final plans and documents with her to ensure that, as his Executor, she would faithfully implement his wishes. A week later, surrounded by Ruth's family and Maggie, Gene died peacefully, secure in his faith that he soon would be joining his beloved Dorothy.

Gene's Memorial Service on January 31, 2009, included the scripture from Second Timothy: 4: 7-8, 18, which well represented his strong faith:

I have fought the good fight,

I have finished the race,

I have kept the faith.

Henceforth there is laid up for me the crown of righteousness,

Which the Lord, the righteous judge

Will award to me on that Day....

The Lord will rescue me from every evil and save me for his Heavenly kingdom.

To him be the glory forever and ever.

Amen

LISTING FOR 'GENE & DOROTHY PROOF PHOTOS

Page #   Identity

p. 12   Alva Allbert

         Louise Allbert

p. 13   Lob House, Raton, NM

p. 14   Eugene Allbert as child

p. 19   Gardiner, NM

p. 21   Eugene Allbert with his parents and Aunt Sadie

p. 22   Eugene Allbert with his parents and Aunt Sadie

p. 23   Allbert family in Blossburg Canyon

p. 24   Allbert boys with Uncle Frank Stevens

p. 25   Beehive coke ovens, Gardiner, NM.

p. 28   Allbert family with Aunt Sadie in Gardiner, NM

p. 30   Raton, NM High School

p. 32   Gene Allbert and Model T car

p. 34   Eugene, Kenneth and Vernon Allbert, 1926

p. 36   David Charles McGrady (on right) with friend?

p. 37   Dorothy's Aunt Margaret Culp McGrady, Uncle Bert's wife.

p. 38   Dorothy McGrady's classroom in Raton, NM

p. 39   Dorothy and friends on picnic in the mountain canyon

p. 40   Dorothy with teacher and classmates

p. 42   Dorothy McGrady typing certificate, 1926

p. 43   Drafting room, Westinghouse, East Pittsburgh

p. 46   Turtle Creek, PA, First Baptist Church

p. 48   Dorothy and Gene on their honeymoon

p. 49   Dorothy and Gene on their honeymoon

p. 51   Gene and Dorothy's first home in Turtle Creek

p. 53   Margaret Louise Allbert (Peggy)

p. 55   Gene and Dorothy with three daughters, Roberta, Ruth and Peggy

p. 57   Ruth and Roberta Allbert, Peggy, Ruth and Roberta Allbert

p. 58   Peggie, Ruth and Roberta Allbert

p. 59   Betty and Al Robinson and daughter, Bobby

p. 61   Roberta, Peggy and Ruth Allbert

p. 62   Betty & Al Robinson, Dorothy Allbert at Lake Erie beach

p. 73   Patent Award to Eugene F. Allbert

p. 78   Dorothy Allbert hanging out the laundry

p. 79   Roberta, Peggy and Ruth Allbert, Raton, NM, 1948

p. 80   Alva, Louise and Dorothy Allbert (back row); Roberta Peggy and Ruth Allbert with dog, Judy (front row) in New Mexico, 1948

p. 82   Roberta, Peggy and Ruth Allbert, Bennett High School students, 1949

p. 83   50th Wedding Anniversary of Alva and Louise Allbert, 1954

p. 84   Eugene, Vernon, Kenneth Allbert (back row); Dorothy, Louise, Alva and Peggy Allbert (middle row); Ruth and Roberta Allbert, (front row) Raton, NM, 1954

p. 137   Gene and Dorothy Allbert at his retirement, 1973

p. 158   "Marriage Buffalo Style", TV Program

p. 160   Dorothy and Eugene's 50th anniversary program

p. 162   Allbert grandchildren at Gene and Dorothy's 50th anniversary: Mark Clarke, Roger E. Dayer, Lawrence Eugene Dayer, David Rogers (top); Stephanie Clarke, Kathleen Clarke, Phyllis Rogers, Mary Ellen Clarke, Cindy Lou Dayer (middle), John Clarke III (in uniform).

p. 163   Delavan Ave. Church friends at Gene & Dorothy's 50th, 1980

Acknowledgments
Gene & Dorothy: A 70 Year Love Story

 I wish to thank my sisters, Margaret Allbert Clarke, and Ruth Allbert Rogers, for sharing family memories with me; our daughter, Cynthia Dayer Erb, for reading an early draft; our son, Larry, for taking photos with his iPhone; and my childhood friend, Roberta Robinson Lawson, for providing family photos and correspondence with my parents. Expert criticism and suggestions came from friends Dianne Bennett, William Graebner and Jane Rube, who carefully read the manuscript and offered trenchant comments and wise suggestions.

 My cheerful publisher, Mary K. Dougherty, has given both moral and practical support as we labored through seemingly endless revisions and corrections. And finally, my husband, Dr. Roger S. Dayer, patiently endured his wife's absence during the long gestation period required for "Gene & Dorothy" to become a reality. Naturally, all errors are my own.

Made in the USA
Middletown, DE
28 December 2016